**DATE DUE**

| | | |
|---|---|---|
| FEB 2 5 | OCT 3 1995 | |
| OCT 6 | | JUL 1 2 2003 |
| 1/13/92 | | |
| AUG 0 6 1993 | | |
| | | |
| OCT 3 0 1993 | | |
| AUG 1 0 1994 | | |
| MAY 1 0 1995 | | |
| JUN 2 6 1995 | | |

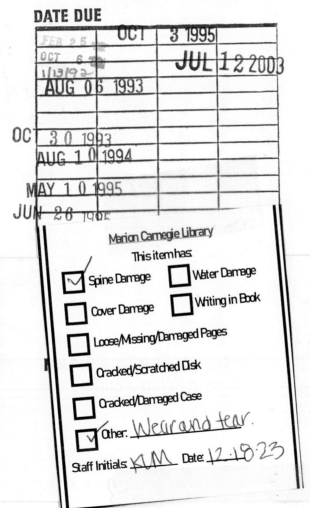

# Jewelry Making

**Dominic DiPasquale** is Associate Professor of Art at the State University of New York, Oswego, and is well known for his creative work in jewelry.

**Jean Delius,** formerly Trustee of the American Crafts Council, is also Associate Professor of Art at S.U.N.Y., Oswego, and an eminent designer of jewelry.

**Thomas C. Eckersley,** who created the photographs for this book, is Assistant Professor of Art at S.U.N.Y., Oswego, and a professional photographer who has exhibited internationally.

DOMINIC DIPASQUALE

JEAN DELIUS / THOMAS ECKERSLEY

# Jewelry Making

## AN ILLUSTRATED GUIDE TO TECHNIQUE

A SPECTRUM BOOK

PRENTICE-HALL, INC., ENGLEWOOD CLIFFS, NEW JERSEY

**Library of Congress Cataloging in Publication Data**

DIPASQUALE, DOMINIC
    Jewelry making.

    (The Creative handcrafts series)    (A Spectrum Book)
    Bibliography:    p.
    1. Jewelry making—Amateurs' manuals. I. Delius,
Jean, joint author. II. Eckersley, Tom, joint author. III.
Title.
TT212.D56        739.27        74-23282
ISBN 0-13-509836-X
ISBN 0-13-509828-9 pbk.

©1975 by Prentice-Hall, Inc.
*Englewood Cliffs, New Jersey*


A SPECTRUM BOOK

10 9 8 7 6 5 4 3 2 1


Printed in the United States of America


Prentice-Hall International, Inc. (*London*)
Prentice-Hall of Australia Pty., Ltd. (*Sydney*)
Prentice-Hall of Canada, Ltd. (*Toronto*)
Prentice-Hall of India Private Limited (*New Delhi*)
Prentice-Hall of Japan, Inc. (*Tokyo*)

In memory of my father, Sebastian, and my brother, Joe;
for Sammy, for much inspiration;
and my sons, Mark and Rory
*D.DiP.*


For Al, Karen, and Cris

*J.M.D.*

# Contents

*Preface*   *ix*

**1**   A Brief Perspective   1

**2**   Design   4

**3**   Tools   11

**4**   Sawing and Piercing   18

**5**   Soldering   21

      EDGE SOLDERING,   23
      SWEAT SOLDERING,   25
      BUTT SOLDERING,   27

**6**   Annealing   30

      ANNEALING WIRE,   32

**7**   Drawing Wire   33

**8**   Jump Rings   35

**9**   Forging   37

**10**  Shaping, Planishing, and Rolling    41

**11**  Disc Cutting and Dapping    45

**12**  Enameling    48

      CLOISONNÉ,    51
      CHAMPLEVÉ,    55
      PLIQUE À JOUR,    58

**13**  Reticulation    61

**14**  Fusing    64

**15**  Etching    68

**16**  Stone Setting    73

      PRONG SETTINGS,    73
      BEZELS,    79

**17**  Hinging    83

**18**  Centrifugal Casting    86

      MODEL MAKING,    86
      SPRUING,    92
      INVESTING,    94
      BURN-OUT,    96
      CASTING,    96

**19**  Finishing    102

      TEXTURING,    109

**20**  Oxidation    110

**21**  Contemporary American Jewelers    112

*Appendix*    *137*

      MELTING POINTS OF NONFERROUS METALS,    137
      APPROXIMATE MELTING POINTS OF SOLDER,    137
      TEMPERATURE CONVERSION,    138
      WEIGHTS AND MEASURES,    138
      CONVERSION OF FRACTIONS AND DECIMALS TO MILLIMETERS,    138
      SPECIFIC GRAVITY OF METALS,    139

*Glossary*    *140*

*Bibliography*    *143*

*Index*    *145*

# Preface

It is hard for us to imagine what life was like just more than a century ago, but consider for a moment not having an automobile, washing machine, power lawn mower, vacuum cleaner, and a list of appliances that could probably fill this page. There is no longer a need for us to go out and chop wood and start a fire in the stove. Now we simply turn a dial and a burner lights up to heat our water. The result of all these mechanical marvels coupled with shorter work weeks adds up to many more leisure hours than people know how to use. Too much of this free time is spent passively before television sets and with other equally unrewarding and meaningless activities. This is contrary to man's very nature. We are born with certain kinesthetic and aesthetic drives and if we are to live happy, healthy lives, we must have outlets to satisfy our creative impulses. The most important ingredient to success is desire. When we want something badly enough, the effort in gaining the achievement becomes as exciting and meaningful as the achievement itself.

A natural avenue that can add meaning to lives overmechanized and systematized is that of the arts. Any number of art forms may appeal to an individual. Theater, for example, offers opportunities for acting, directing, and dance. There are many other related fields of interest, however, such as stage design, lighting, costuming, choreography, and so on. Creative writing, painting, sculpture, and printmaking are other areas that offer opportunities for expression. Currently, the greatest interest lies in the crafts. They include woodworking, glassblowing, textiles, ceramics, and the subject of this book, jewelry.

Making jewelry by hand has enjoyed a renaissance in this country since World War II. This is largely because colleges and universities throughout the nation have recognized the need for more creative activity by the student, and have subsequently developed craft programs and more art electives as part of their curricula. Many fine European craftsmen have been encouraged to come to the United States to teach the craft, and many European shows of jewelry and metalwork have toured the country. Magazines such as *Craft Horizons* have emerged and developed a large following. Craft organizations have sprung up at regional, state, and national levels. Most of them have sponsored annual competitions and exhibitions, as do some of the finest museums and galleries in the country. All this has done a great deal to encourage active involvement in jewelry making and the other crafts as well.

This book is directed toward two separate audiences. The first is the beginning jewelry class in college, university, or high school. It is intended to help the instructor by freeing much of the time he has had to spend on fundamental techniques, enabling him to work with his students on an individual basis and deal with the problems of aesthetics, design, and of course the more involved technical problems that may arise with a particular design.

Hobbyists will also find this book most helpful. Because it is so completely illustrated, it should serve as a silent instructor.

There are more techniques and methods used in jewelry making than in any of the other crafts. As was previously mentioned, this book deals with the fundamentals of this art form. There are other methods of approaching many of the problems illustrated here, and many techniques that have not been touched on, for to do so would result in literally volumes of work. Hopefully, however, this one book is complete enough to kindle an interest and personal involvement that may make your leisure time (or working time, if you have chosen this as a career) more meaningful and pleasant for you.

# 1 A Brief Perspective

As far back as we can trace, man has been concerned with the art of personal adornment. Decorating and adorning his body has always been a part of culture.

In primitive societies this inclination was often first evidenced in body painting, tattooing, and scarification, all of which are still practiced by aboriginal tribes today. Earliest evidences of painted or marked human skin have been found on Egyptian mummies dating back to 2000 B.C. Tattooing existed in Japan as early as the sixth century B.C. and was probably brought from Asia to the South Sea Islands at an early date. Most motifs used in body painting and tattooing were related to magical or puberty rites at first; only many centuries later did they become purely decorative. Facial tattooing was practiced almost solely by those of high birth because of its cost, and came to be a recognized sign of caste. Complete body tattooing, because of the pain of its execution, was used to designate bravery, and those of warrior status sported the most elaborate body tattoos. Although tattooing was practiced by Ancient Britons, Thracians, Gauls, and Germans, it virtually disappeared with the rise of Christianity. However, as Western European navigators explored and charted the world from the fifteenth century onward, tattooing became a sailor's art and was soon popularized at home as the decorated sailors returned from their voyages. The word "tattoo" was derived from the Tahitian "tatau," meaning "to mark," and the

7/7/94

practice spread as explorers brought home and exhibited natives of the South Seas with total body tattoos. Early explorers of the Western Hemisphere reported that the natives there also displayed tattoos, and American Indians painted their bodies before going into battle. By the nineteenth century it had become a popular art and remained so until World War I.

The fashioning of objects to adorn the body is almost as old as direct decoration of the body. The rarity of gold made it precious, and its malleability made it an ideal material for objects of sacred and ritual use. The great gold treasures of the ancient Celts, Egyptians, Greeks, pre-Columbian Americans, and other ancient peoples, housed in museums throughout the world, tell us much about these cultures and their concern for personal adornment.

Jewelry has played many roles throughout history. For nomadic peoples it was a way of carrying their assets with them always. The amount of jewelry worn by members of a tribe or family was an indication of its wealth and status.

Precious metals and gemstones are the traditional materials of jewelry and until recently, with the development of a mass-production costume jewelry industry, only those objects employing materials of great intrinsic worth were considered true jewels. Today the emphasis has shifted from gold, silver, platinum, and an ostentatious display of gems to a concern for design with any material. We now see fine jewelry employing iron, steel, brass, plastic, fibers, feathers, and glass—often in direct juxtaposition to the precious metals and stones.

Jewelry as a status symbol has its roots in economics. Wealth was almost exclusively in the hands of the ruling class and the Church until the early sixteenth century, which saw the beginning of the rise of a middle class of merchants. Until then, royalty and church hierarchy were the great patrons, commissioning the works we see today in the museums of the world. With the growth of a wealthy merchant class desirous of emulating the life style of their "betters," however, jewelers found an almost insatiable market for their finest and most expensive work. To own and wear jewels as fine as those royalty owned was an overt manifestation of a growing power in a new social structure.

As mass-production methods and new, inexpensive materials and paste stones were developed in the nineteenth century, more and more wage-earners could aspire to the adornments heretofore reserved for only those of great wealth, and in the Western world jewelry became an indication of the upward mobility of the masses. Low-cost white metal castings and synthetic stones made it difficult for any but the experts to determine social position by a cursory examination of an individual's "jewels."

With the wars and social upheavals of the first half of the twentieth century, the increasing disillusionment with the mechanization and anonymity within our society, and the search for a more personal and individual identity, the role of the individual craftsman, designing and making a unique product, has assumed a new importance. More leisure time afforded by the efforts of organized labor in decreasing the hours of work, providing greater income and far higher levels of education for more people, have created a vastly expanded interest in all the crafts, not only as consumer products but as avenues of creation as well. The pioneering efforts of the American Crafts Council in the past thirty years have established an ambience in which the craftsman can live and work with dignity as well as with an unparalleled demand for his products.

All of these circumstances have combined to make the contemporary jeweler the social and economic counterpart of his Renaissance forebear. The point at which he departs from his ties with the past is in his totally individual approach to the design of his work, his lack of concern for using only traditional materials. Unique, craftsman-created jewelry today becomes a statement about the maker as well as an adornment for the wearer, and creates a link between the two.

The successful piece of jewelry may serve a variety of roles for the wearer, complementing a special outfit, designating an office or societal position, announcing an engagement (or even, by omission, suggesting the availability of an individual for marriage), as well as conveying austerity, frivolity, innovation, or lack of concern for tradition. The sexual role of jewelry might be likened to the plumage of birds, the change in coloration of animals and fish at periods of sexual receptivity, or the characteristic specialized movements of animals in mating activity. Jewelry may be used to attract members of the opposite sex. It becomes an extension of the personality of the wearer and, as such, is a method of communication to the viewer—an indication of his or her desires.

Simultaneously with an increased consumer interest in the products of the craftsman has come a vastly increased interest in the processes of creation of these new art objects. One need only visit any of the many craft fairs and festivals springing up all over the country to see the tremendous public interest in the demonstrations and the avid attention paid to the craftsman at work. Adult and continuing education classes, community center classes, museum classes, craftsmen teaching in their studios as well as in universities, even tool and material supply houses instituting classes for their customers, all testify to the rapidly burgeoning interest in learning to do, to participate personally in the creative process. Publishers' lists of new books contain an ever-growing number of volumes aimed at filling the public's seemingly insatiable desire to work actively in the various craft media, with jewelry making high on the list. The technical knowledge necessary is eminently learnable and it is the intention of this book to make it pleasurable and logical and thus to introduce the joy and excitement of creating unique jewelry to the increasingly interested public.

Cast ring, sterling silver with cultured
pearl. Design derived from underwater
plant life.
Mary Ann Spavins*

# 2 Design

The real joy and satisfaction associated with jewelry making is achieved with the
creation of new designs. Virtually anyone can learn the methods and techniques
used in jewelry making and, provided he possesses a reasonable amount of pa-
tience and determination, he will be able to develop these skills to a professional
level of craftsmanship.

The key to success in jewelry making is in design, for no matter how well a
piece is crafted, if it is not well-designed the result will not be successful. This is
not to suggest that good design is more important than good craftsmanship, for a
piece that is well-designed and poorly crafted will also be considered a failure.
Obviously, both are necessary to achieve success. But because design precedes
execution in jewelry making, it becomes the primary consideration.

An important step in developing good design is to become acquainted with
what is being done and what has been done in jewelry as well as other areas of
the arts. When you visit an exhibition or see jewelry and other art objects in
books and periodicals, you should look at them analytically. When you see
something you like, you should ask yourself why you like it. What are the
qualities that most appeal to you? Is it the form, texture, lineal quality, sim-
plicity, complexity, color, grace, angularity? Most likely, those qualities that
appeal to you most will have a direct influence on your own designing.

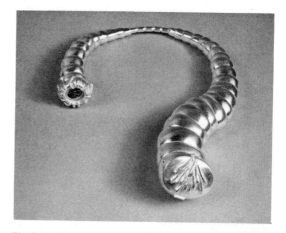

Fig. 2.1  Fused pendant, sterling silver.  Design suggested by onion shape.
Dominic DiPasquale

Fig. 2.2  Neck piece, sterling silver and abalone.  Hollow constructed form suggested by sea-life forms and shells.
Mary Ann Spavins*

Any shape or shapes you choose to build your design with may have been used countless times before. Your search will be for new relationships and effects of these motifs in your effort to make a personal statement.

The most common way to approach the designing of jewelry is by sketching. An ability to draw is desirable but not essential, because the drawing of pictures is not at all like sketching for jewelry design. You may use any device such as a compass. ruler, or french curve if it will help you reach for an idea. When a design shows promise but is not entirely satisfactory, cover it with tracing paper, trace the good portions, and rework those parts that disturb you. Do this as often as necessary to solve the problems of a particular design.

Fig. 2.3  Cast and constructed ring, sterling silver with baroque pearl.  Pearl form sets mood for the metal.
Jean Delius
Fig. 2.4  Cast ring, 14K yellow gold with topaz quartz. Conscious use of organic form as contrast to geometric faceted stone.
Darlene Benzon*

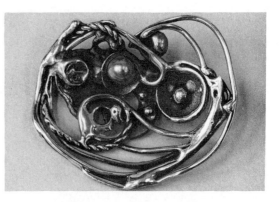

Fig. 2.5  Cast ring, sterling silver with amethyst.
Organic form develops from shank and grows to high
crown which holds stone.
Mary Ann Spavins*

Fig. 2.6  Cast pin, sterling silver with black baroque
pearl. Fluidity of molten metal during casting process
is emphasized by finished piece.
Jean Delius

You may begin by working thoughtfully—that is, by predetermining in your
mind the shape you wish to draw. Another method is the intuitive approach, in
which you let the pencil discover shapes by moving it freely over the paper, then
selecting those you feel show the most promise. The thought process then takes
over as you decide to reduce or enlarge shapes to achieve better proportions, to
introduce line, texture, a three-dimensional quality, or any idea you feel will
enhance your design. Remember that you are searching for an unknown. Rarely
will an idea occur to you that you will not be able to improve upon. It is well
worth the effort to find the best solution of which you are capable.

Cutting paper is another approach to design. When shapes are cut out of

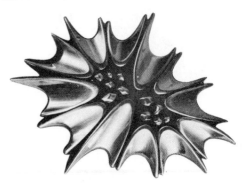

Fig. 2.7  Fused pendant, sterling silver. Design based on
foaming crest of an ocean wave.
Jean Delius

Fig. 2.8  Constructed pin, sterling silver. Design derived
from abstraction reflecting a floral concept.
Dominic DiPasquale

Fig. 2.9  Forged and cast neck piece, sterling silver with black opals.  Abstraction of an angel with outstretched wings.
Dominic DiPasquale

Fig. 2.10  Cast ring, 14K yellow gold. Graceful and repetitious form derived geometrically.
Lucille Bartlett*

Fig. 2.12  Hollow constructed ring, sterling silver with black onyx. Development of ring shank to triangular forms of top and·stone creates a unity of total form.
Dominic DiPasquale

Fig. 2.13  Cast ring, sterling silver with aquamarine.  Soaring aerodynamic forms rise to hold stone.
Dominic DiPasquale

Fig. 2.14  Hollow constructed ring, sterling silver.  Sharply incised geometric decoration is used as contrast to convex form.
Mary Ann Spavins*

Fig. 2.11  Constructed ring, sterling silver with fire opal. Simple rising form accentuated by toothed bezel.
Dominic DiPasquale

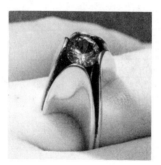

7

Design

Fig. 2.15 Fused pendant, sterling silver. Random arrangement of silver scrap forms basis for this design. Mary Ann Spavins*

Fig. 2.16 Fused pendant sterling silver. As opposed to figure 2.15, this design employs a more consciously ordered arrangement of curved scrap forms. Dominic DiPasquale

paper (preferably construction paper), they can be moved and shifted easily in an effort to find the best relationships. By folding the paper several times and cutting it, you can create symmetrical designs ranging from very simple to very complex. Beyond this, when the paper is bent, folded, twisted, curled, etc., it emphasizes the three-dimensional aspect of jewelry design.

Designs need not be totally the product of your imagination. Nature, for example, provides an endless source of inspiration for design. Natural forms, however, should not be imitated but rather serve as a point of departure upon which you can create a design. Take a more careful look at leaves and their structure, flowers, twigs, the grain in various woods, snails, shells, fish, birds,

Fig. 2.17 Cast and hinged hand ornament, sterling silver with amethyst crystal. Structural plains of uncut amethyst crystal are reflected in the metal forms to achieve unity of design. Mary Ann Spavins*

Fig. 2.18 Constructed ring, 14K yellow gold with rutilated smoky quartz. To give the very large stone a feeling of floating above the hand, an absolute minimum of ring structure is used. Jean Delius

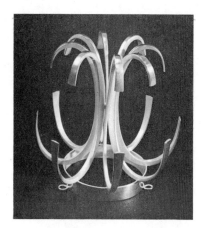

Fig. 2.19 Forged and constructed bridal crown, sterling silver. Design inspired by spouting water fountain. Dominic DiPasquale

Fig. 2.20 Cast and constructed ring, sterling silver with moss agate. Cast form is suggestive of swirling moss forms within stone and further reinforced by spinning stone, which is pivoted in setting. Mary Ann Spavins*

Fig. 2.21 Repousséd, chased, and constructed pendant, sterling silver. The world of mythology and fantasy inspired this design. Barbara Gemza*

Fig. 2.22 Cast ring, sterling silver. Personal interests can inspire design as in this comedy-tragedy ring. Nilgin Sari*

feathers, cloud formations, fruits and vegetables, animal and insect forms. This list can be extended significantly and each item is capable of stimulating countless ideas for design.

Manmade objects may be used in much the same way. Such things as musical instruments, telephones, gears, boats, machines, pulleys, tools, etc., can provide the same kind of stimulus for design.

Another ageless source of design is found in geometric forms such as circles, squares, triangles, trapezoids, and rectangles in varying sizes and used in combination.

The practicality of a design is an important consideration. Try to avoid sharp pointed edges that may catch on clothing and result in damage to the piece of jewelry, and possibly scratch the wearer or people who come into contact with the wearer.

Fig. 2.23  Constructed bridal crown, sterling silver. Lace effect of filigree design intended to relate to the delicate fabric of a wedding gown. Dominic DiPasquale

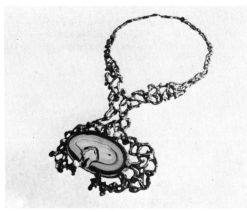

Fig. 2.24  Cast neck piece, sterling silver with agate. Organic form emphasizes the natural pattern of the stone. Mary Ann Spavins*

Earrings, particularly those made for pierced ears, should be light in weight; objects like belt buckles should be made of a gauge of metal that is strong enough to stand up to the pressure of a Thanksgiving dinner.

When you design jewelry for a particular person, take into consideration the person's size and use proportions that will be complementary for that individual. The person's personality is also important. A shy or conservative person will want designs quite different from those that attract an outgoing, flamboyant person.

The suggestions made in this chapter merely scratch the surface for approaches to design. The methods you use may be inspired by other means, but most important is that the approach you use is one that has meaning to you. This is essential if your designs are going to reflect your feelings and develop into a personal statement.

# 3 Tools

The care and maintenance of tools is vitally important to the craftsman because the condition of his tools bears a direct relationship to the quality of his craftsmanship. When certain precautions are taken, the tools will always be ready for use when needed.

There are several kinds of hammers used in jewelry making. Some of them,

Fig. 3.1 Jeweler's saw frame and enlarged saw blade showing proper relationship of blade to frame.

Fig. 3.2 Bottom Row: hand file, pillar file half-round, four assorted needle files. Second row: eight assorted needle files. Top row: emery stick, all resting on emery board made by cementing emery cloth to plywood.

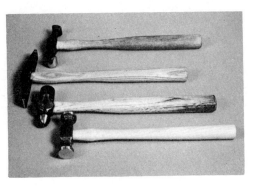

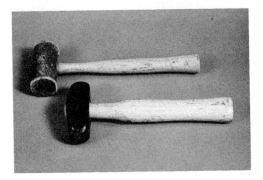

Fig. 3.3 Jeweler's pliers starting at 10 o'clock: round-nose parallel, flat-nose parallel, chain-nose, half-round, end cutters, side cutters, round-nose.

Fig. 3.4 Hammers from top: forming, cross peen, ball peen, planishing.

Fig. 3.5 Rawhide mallet, forging hammer.

Fig. 3.6 Hollow ground scraper, curved burnisher, chasing tools, chasing hammer.

Fig. 3.7 From top: third arm with pointed cross-locking tweezer, enameling tweezer, soldering tweezer, blunt-nose cross-locking tweezer.

Fig. 3.8 Soldering torch for natural gas and compressed air, striker.

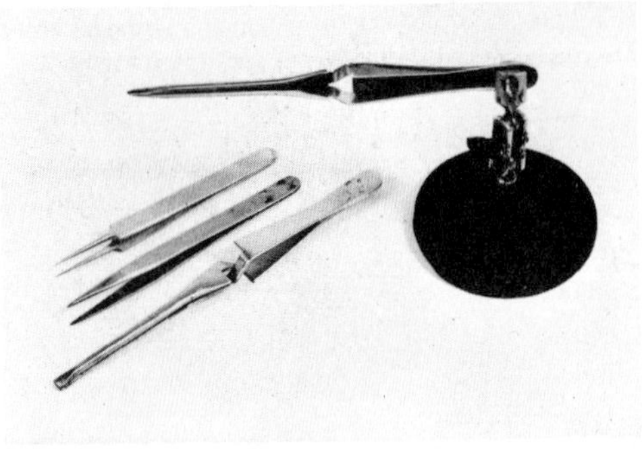

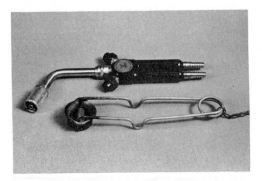

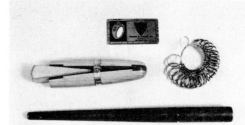

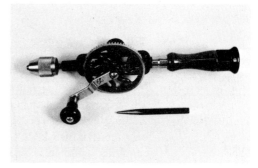

Fig. 3.9 Annealing pan with pumice pebbles, asbestos soldering pad on turntable.

Fig. 3.10 Top: ring size-measuring gauge. Middle: ring clamp, ring sizes. Bottom: mandrel.

Fig. 3.11 Hand drill, center punch.

Fig. 3.12 Pickle pot.
Fig. 3.13 Small adjustable bench vise.
Fig. 3.14 Vise.

13

Fig. 3.15 Flat T-stake in stake plate.

Fig. 3.16 From left: oval mushroom stake, spoon stake in stake holder, round mushroom stake, blowhorn.

such as the planishing and forming hammers, have highly polished faces and are used to smooth and shape the softer nonferrous metals. When the face of a planishing hammer becomes nicked, the nick will be reproduced in the metal each time it is struck. It is important, therefore, to keep the hammer face as smooth and polished as possible. Hammers used for this purpose should never be used for striking center punches or chasing tools or anything made of iron or steel. To prevent damage to hammer faces as a result of careless storage, racks and hangers should be constructed to keep them organized and protected. Ball peen and chasing hammers are used with center punches and chasing tools.

Forming stakes are frequently the recipients of misdirected hammer blows and also become marred. When this occurs, the stake should be refinished and kept polished for best results in forming and planishing.

Rust is the mortal enemy of tools. When pliers, cutters, dividers, etc., are left where water can get into the hinge, rust will develop and seriously impair the

Fig. 3.17 Curved T-stake.

Fig. 3.18 Fluting stake.

Fig. 3.19  Assortment of stakes and
mandrels, stake holders.

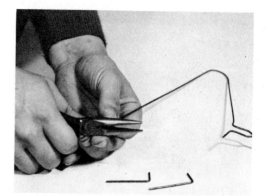

Fig. 3.20  Supports made from wire
coat hanger.

function of the tool if not render it totally useless. If this does occur, the tool should be soaked in a solution of 50 percent kerosene and 50 percent gasoline overnight and then wire brushed.

Humidity creates some of the same problems. When tools are exposed to an unusually high degree of humidity, particularly when they are not used for a period of time, they can be protected with a thin coat of petroleum jelly and a drop of machine oil on moving parts.

Saw frames should not be stored with saw blades under tension. This tends to weaken both the frame and the blade.

Files should always be protected from touching each other in storage, because the rubbing of one file against another will result in the dulling of both files.

Most often, tools that are damaged can be restored to working condition, but this takes time away from creative endeavor. It's the old story about an ounce of prevention being worth a pound of cure.

Fig. 3.21  Assortment of draw plates
and draw tongs.

Fig. 3.22  Tube cutter.

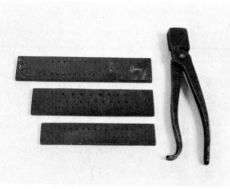

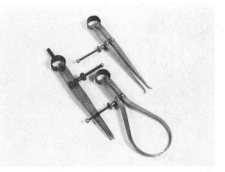

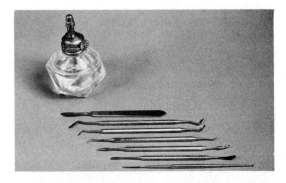

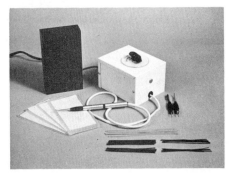

Fig. 3.23   From left:  dividers, outside calipers, inside calipers.

Fig. 3.24   Alcohol lamp, assortment of dental wax tools.

Fig. 3.25   Clockwise from 10 o'clock:  hard carving wax, electric waxing tool and tips, assorted wax wires, sheet wax.

Fig. 3.26   Centrifugal casting machine mounted in steel drum.

Fig. 3.27   Burn-out kiln.

Fig. 3.28   Scotch stone, agate mortar and pestle.

Fig. 3.29   Buffing compounds.  Top:  diamond white; left, green rouge; right, tripoli.

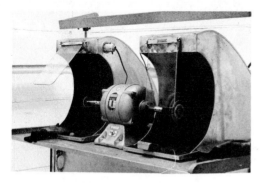

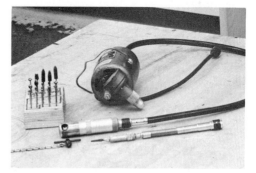

Fig. 3.30   Top: assorted goblet buffs.
Bottom: muslin buffing wheels.

Fig. 3.32   Buffing machine with two
tapered spindles and shields.

Fig. 3.31   Brass wire goblet buff,
brass wire wheel.

Fig. 3.33   Flexible shaft with
accessories.

Fig. 3.34   Engraver's ball and leather
pad.

Fig. 3.35   Rolling mill.

# 4 Sawing and Piercing

Perhaps the most basic skill the jeweler must master is that of sawing. With the proper approach and a little practice, you will find that this is a realatively simple operation.

The first step for the preparation of sawing is to place the design to be cut clearly on the metal. This is best accomplished by drawing the design on tracing paper, painting rubber cement lightly on both the back of the drawing and the metal, waiting a few moments for the cement to dry, and carefully smoothing the paper on the metal.

Fig. 4.1 A light coat of rubber cement has been applied to both metal and drawing and allowed to air-dry. Drawing is now carefully adhered to metal and smoothed down.

Fig. 4.2 Internal piercing will be sawed out first. Holes to be drilled are first center-punched to guide drill bit.

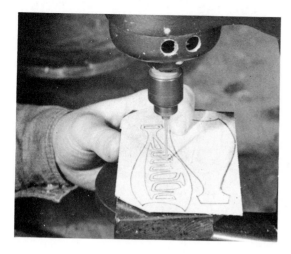

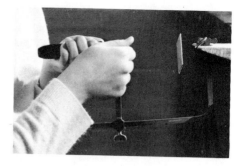

Fig. 4.4, Metal is threaded on saw blade.

Fig. 4.3 With a small bit, hole is drilled for saw blade.

The saw blade should be placed in the saw frame with the teeth facing out and down (see fig. 4.5, below). Enough tension should be placed on the saw blade so that when it is plucked like a guitar string it will make a musical note. A dull sound indicates that there is not enough tension on the blade.

Jeweler's benches are 36 inches high and the stools are generally adjustable. The stool should be set at the lowest position for sawing to permit the arm to move freely. It is most important that the saw frame be held in as vertical a position as possible. The metal is placed on the bench pin and held firmly, with the thumb and fingers acting as a clamp. Very little forward pressure is required to cut the metal. The hand holding the saw frame guides the saw blade along the pencil line. Rather than turning the blade in the direction of the line, turn the metal as you continue to saw so that the line you are cutting is always facing

Fig. 4.6 Saw frame is held in a relaxed upright position with the jeweler sitting low at the bench to allow for greatest freedom of arm movement.

Fig. 4.5 Blade is tightened under tension in bottom of saw frame.

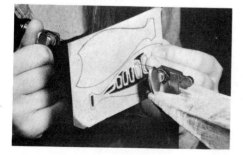

19

straight away from the blade. It is possible to cut extremely sharp angles and very intricate designs using this approach.

Piercing is accomplished by first drilling a hole through the metal. To prevent the drill bit from drifting, mark the position of the hole with a center punch. After drilling the hole with a small drill bit, place the saw blade firmly in the top end of the saw frame, put the blade through the hole in the metal, and secure

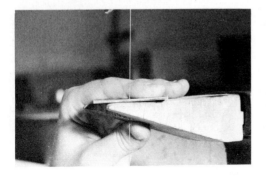

Fig. 4.7  Metal is held firmly to bench pin with fingers and thumb while sawing.

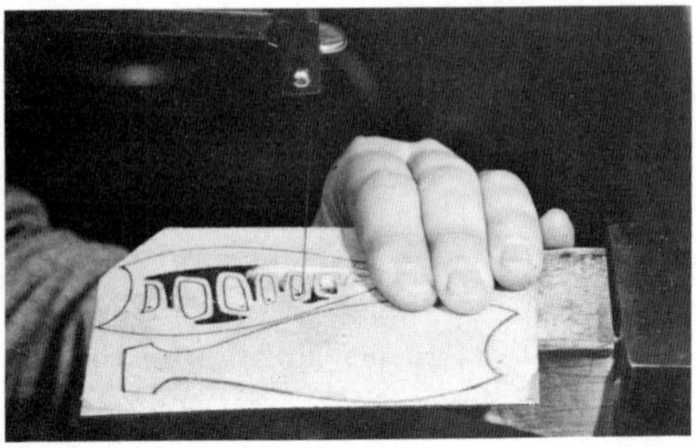

Fig. 4.8  Pencil line of design is followed, the metal is gently turned as the saw moves so that blade is always guided forward along line.

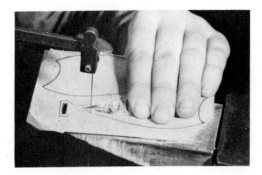

Fig. 4.9  After internal piercing is complete, the outline of form is sawed, following line as before.

the blade in the bottom of the frame. Then proceed with the sawing. When a design has internal piercing, it is always best to saw the pierced areas first. It is easier to hold the larger piece of metal while sawing these openings.

Saw blades break most frequently as a result of holding the saw frame at an angle, turning the metal too abruptly, using too much forward pressure, or not holding the metal firmly enough against the bench pin.

# 5 Soldering

Soldering, or the joining of pieces of metal, is a basic technique that must be mastered by the jewelry student. It is a skill that is learned through experience. The more you practice soldering, the sooner you will be able to sense where to apply the flame, what intensity of heat is required, and when the solder will flow.

The materials and equipment necessary for soldering are as follows:

TORCH. There are many types of torches available that are effective in soldering precious metals together.

1. Natural gas and compressed air—the torch used in the demonstrations throughout this book.

2. Propane torch—commonly used in soldering; relatively inexpensive and available at most hardware stores.

3. Acetylene torch—produces a hotter flame than propane torches and is particularly desirable in melting metal for casting.

4. Natural gas and oxygen—produces a much hotter flame and is capable of soldering platinum.

TURNTABLE OR ANNEALING PAN.    When the piece being soldered is placed on a turntable or annealing pan, all parts of the piece can be reached by turning the table instead of moving the torch around the piece.

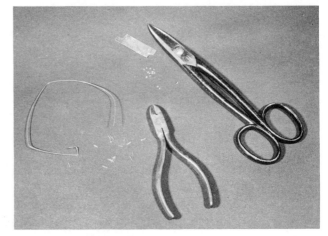

Fig. 5.1 Sheet solder is cut in 1/16″ square pellets with plate shears. Wire solder is cut in 1/8″ lengths with diagonal cutters.

ASBESTOS BOARD.   Asbestos board is sometimes used as a surface upon which to solder and generally as a protective surface for the workbench.

CHARCOAL BLOCK.   Used as a surface to solder on, the charcoal block tends to retain and reflect heat, thus speeding the soldering operation.

SOLDERING TWEEZERS.   This tool is used to pick up and apply solder pellets to the work.

SOLDERING PICK.   The soldering pick is also used to pick up solder pellets by moistening the end with flux; it also pushes the pieces of solder back in place if the heating causes them to move.

FLUX. There are paste and liquid fluxes available. Each enjoys certain advantages over the other. Both are effective, and experimentation with each of them is encouraged to determine your preference. All of the demonstrations in this book have been performed with paste flux.

SOLDER. Silver solder is used to solder silver, copper, and brass. It is available in both sheet and wire form. The sheet solder is cut with plate shears into pellets of about 1/16-inch square. Wire solder is generally cut approximately 1/8-inch long.

Silver solder comes in four grades, each with its own melting point (see table, on p. 137). The jeweler need only concern himself with three of the grades: hard, medium, and easy. When it is necessary to solder several times on the same piece, you should start with the hard solder and work down to easy so previously soldered joints will not reflow.

Gold solder is available in sheet form and should be used according to the karat of gold to be soldered.

YELLOW OCHRE.   Mixed to a tempera-paint consistency and applied to a joint that has been soldered, yellow ochre is an insulating material that will prevent solder from reflowing. It is particularly useful when there are many soldered joints on a single piece.

THIRD ARM.   A third arm is a weighted adjustable stand that holds a cross-locking tweezer which in turn is used to hold a piece of metal in place while it is being soldered.

COAT-HANGER WIRE.     Cut to 3- to 4-inch lengths and bent into right angles to prevent them from rolling, coat-hanger wire is used to support the piece being soldered so that the heat from the torch can circulate more freely around the piece.

Although there are several approaches to soldering, there are certain basic procedures that must be observed in order to insure success.

1. The pieces to be soldered together must be thoroughly cleaned, particularly where the metal is to be joined. This may be accomplished by rubbing the surfaces with very fine emery cloth or steel wool. Avoid touching the surfaces with your fingers once they have been cleaned.

2. The pieces that are to be soldered together must be touching. This is vitally important because although solder makes an extremely strong joint, it does not serve well as a filler. It is also important in terms of conducting heat between the pieces to be soldered so they will reach the melting point of the solder simultaneously, thus causing the solder to flow into the joint.

3. The pieces must be fluxed at the points that are to be soldered. Flux will prevent the metal from oxidizing and ease the flow of the solder.

4. Solder pellets must be applied.

5. Solder flows because the metal on which the solder lays reaches the melting point of the solder. For this reason, the torch flame is directed to the metal and not to the solder pellets. The size of the torch flame should be proportionate to the size of the pieces of metal to be soldered together. Fine wire will require a small delicate flame, while sheet silver will require a larger and hotter flame. When a small piece of metal is soldered to a larger piece, the heat should first be concentrated on the larger piece because it will need more heat to bring it to the melting point of the solder.

## EDGE SOLDERING

The approach to soldering will vary according to the needs of a particular design. The first demonstration is of edge soldering. The following procedure is recommended to achieve an invisible joint. The upper shape is cut to the precise line of the design. The lower shape is cut 1/16-inch larger all around than the upper

Fig. 5.2  Both surfaces to be soldered are coated with flux.

Fig. 5.3  Fluxed pieces are laid on supports on charcoal block and heated until flux becomes glassy.

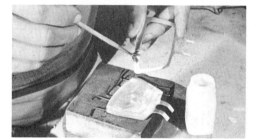

Fig. 5.4 Solder pellets are applied to edge with soldering pick.

shape to provide an edge on which to place the solder. The surfaces to be soldered together are cleaned with a piece of worn 320 emery cloth. The lower shape is placed on supports made of coat-hanger wire. Flux is applied to the surfaces that are to be soldered together and the upper shape is put in place. The flux is heated until it stops boiling and appears glassy on the surface of the metal. The pellets of solder are then moistened with flux and placed all around the protruding edge.

The piece is now ready to be soldered. The temperature of both pieces of metal must reach the melting point of the solder at the same time. To accomplish this, heat the piece generally at first, then concentrate the heat on the heavier piece of metal, because it will require more heat than the smaller piece to reach the soldering temperature simultaneously. When the solder starts to flow, direct the flame on the joint and rotate the turntable so the solder will flow around the joint.

If any additional soldering is required, the soldered edge may reflow. For this reason, the protruding edge should not be cut off until all soldering is completed.

Fig. 5.5 Heat is directed under and around lower piece until solder flows around the joint.

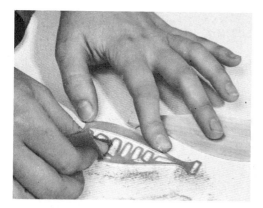

Fig. 5.6 Surfaces to be soldered together are cleaned with emery cloth.

Fig. 5.7 Surfaces to be soldered together are fluxed.

## SWEAT SOLDERING

The second demonstration is of sweat soldering. This method gives a stronger bond and is necessary here because the metal will be shaped. Both surfaces must fit together perfectly. Again, as in edge soldering, the upper shape is cut to the precise line of the design and the lower piece is cut 1/16-inch larger to insure an invisible joint. The bottom side of the upper piece and the top side of the lower piece are cleaned with fine emery cloth, fluxed, and heated until the flux becomes glassy. Solder pellets are applied to the fluxed surface of the upper piece and flowed with the torch. The upper piece is then placed in position on the fluxed surface of the lower piece, which is raised from the surface of the char-

Fig. 5.8 After heating flux to a glassy surface solder pellets are applied to back of top piece.

25

Fig. 5.9 Solder is heated until it begins to flow.

Fig. 5.10 Pieces are placed together on supports on charcoal block.

coal block with supports so that the torch flame can be flashed under the piece, concentrating heat on the larger piece of metal. When the lower piece reaches the flow point of the solder, the upper piece will sink to the surface of the lower piece and the solder will appear as a bright silver line around the entire joint.

Figs. 5.11, 5.12 Heat is flashed beneath and around bottom piece until solder reflows and shows as a bright silver line around the joint.

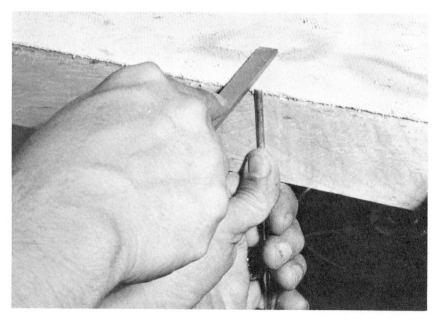

Fig. 5.13  Butt edge is filed perfectly flat against edge of work-bench.

## BUTT SOLDERING

Ring bands, bezels, and bangle bracelets are among the things that are butt soldered. It is imperative that the joint to be soldered be filed to a perfect fit. This may be done by placing the edge of the metal perpendicular to the work-bench surface and filing the edge flat with a smooth, even, forward stroke. This

Fig. 5.14  Size of ring is marked for cutting, sawed and filed as above.

Fig. 5.15  Ends are brought together with half-round pliers to form an ellipse.

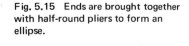

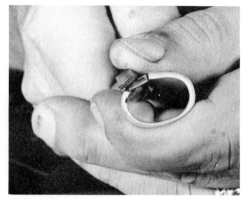

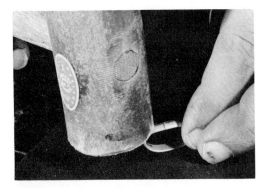

Fig. 5.16 Ends are forced together
under tension by striking with a leather
mallet.

Fig. 5.17 After piece is fluxed, heated
solder pellets are laid along the joint
and soldered.

Fig. 5.18 Piece is laid horizontally on
charcoal block and heat is used to draw
solder through joint.

is repeated on the opposite edge. Bring the ends together in an oval shape so the
edges meet perfectly. Final shaping should take place after the soldering. The
ring band is held with a third arm and cross-locking tweezer. Apply the flux to
the joint and heat until glassy. Lay the solder pellets along the seam and heat
until solder flows. Place band horizontally on charcoal block and heat from
inside to draw the solder through the seam.

Fig. 5 19 Band is opened by striking on
end with leather mallet.

Fig. 5.20 Opened band is shaped on
ring mandrel with leather mallet.

Fig. 5.21 Perfect circle is obtained by striking lightly with a planishing hammer over the ring mandrel. This method may also be used to stretch the ring band to a larger size.

Fig. 5.22 Finished ring band.

## SOLDERING FINDINGS

Locate the position of the findings on the back of the piece. Apply flux *very* sparingly at these points and at the bottom of the findings. Place findings in position and heat the piece until flux becomes glassy. If findings move, push them back in place with a soldering pick. Place a small pellet of easy solder at the base of the findings and apply heat to the piece, *not* on the findings!

After each soldering operation, the piece should be immersed in heated pickle to remove flux residue and any oxides that may have formed on the surface of the piece.

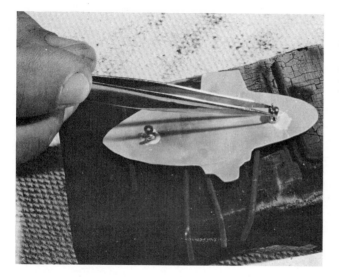

Fig. 5.23 Findings are placed in position on fluxed spots and heated until flux is glassy. This adheres findings in place temporarily. Solder pellets are placed around findings and heat is concentrated on the piece *NOT* findings, until solder flows.

29

# 6 Annealing

Sterling silver is one of the most malleable of all metals. It can be shaped and fashioned into any number of compound curves and forms. This shaping is accomplished by raising and planishing the metal over metal forms called stakes with a variety of hammers. This action tempers the metal, because it compresses the molecules and leaves the metal hard and springy. The annealing process relaxes the molecules and makes the silver malleable again so that it can be worked further. Annealing silver also affects the metal in another way. Bear in mind that the sterling silver that is commonly used is an alloy of 92.5 percent pure or fine silver and 7.5 percent copper. The alloy of the two metals results in a much stronger material than silver in its pure form and is therefore much more durable. When sterling is annealed the first time, it will turn a dark cherry-red color, and when the heat is removed a black scale will have formed on the surface of the metal. This scale is the residue of the copper that was on the surface of the metal. When it is placed in the pickling solution for several minutes, the scale will disappear and leave the metal with a coat of fine silver on the surface. Each time the metal is annealed, the fine silver surface is built up further. The annealing process is important in forming metal, in enameling, and in finishing.

To anneal silver, place the metal in an annealing pan filled with pumice

Fig. 6.1 Place metal in annealing pan and apply soft flame until metal glows dark cherry-red.

Fig. 6.2 As heat is removed a dark scale will form on surface of metal.

stones. Apply a relatively soft flame; that is, a flame that consists of less air and more gas than one that is used in soldering. Heat the entire piece slowly and evenly, turning the annealing pan at the same time so as to reach the entire piece. Bring the metal to a dark cherry-red color. Bright red is too hot and will change the molecular structure of the metal. Immerse the metal in the pickle solution to remove the scale that has formed on the surface. If annealing becomes necessary a second or third time, it is important to look for a different effect on the metal. Because the copper has been removed from the surface, it will no longer turn dark cherry-red. When the proper annealing temperature is reached, a whitish haze will form on the metal.

Fig. 6.3 Metal is immersed in heated pickle to remove scale.

Fig. 6.4 As annealing process is repeated, a haze will form on surface of metal, replacing fire scale.

Fig. 6.5 Wire is coiled and wound with binding wire in preparation for annealing.

Fig. 6.6 Coiled wire is place on asbestos pad and annealed with soft flame.

## ANNEALING WIRE

Because wire is long and thin, it will absorb heat unevenly. Part of the wire may melt while part may not be sufficiently annealed. To avoid this, wire should be wound into a coil and bound with binding wire. Then proceed with the annealing in the same manner as for annealing sheet metal. **Remove the binding wire before immersing it in the pickle solution.**

# 7 Drawing Wire

Wire is available in several gauges, but there are times when a craftsman will require a gauge of wire that is not commercially available. When that is the case, wire may be extruded through draw plates to achieve the desired gauge.

The end of the wire is filed to a long tapering point. The draw plate is placed

Fig. 7.1   A piece of wire no less than 4 inches or more than 2 feet is cut.

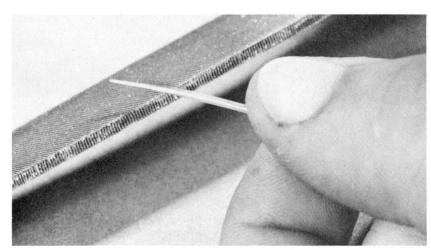

Fig. 7.2  End of wire is filed to a long tapered point.

in a vise and the wire put through the first hole that offers resistance. The wire is then drawn through the plate with a pair of draw tongs. This is repeated until the desired gauge is reached.

The wire will stretch in length as it is drawn thinner. The drawing process also compresses the molecules of the metal, thus tempering the wire. It may be necessary to anneal the wire, depending on how many times it will be drawn through the plate.

Draw plates are available for all shapes of wire.

Fig. 7.3  Wire is placed from rear of plate through first hole that offers resistance.  End of wire is grasped with draw tongs and pulled steadily through plate.

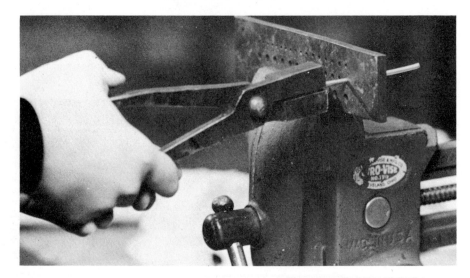

# $8$ Jump Rings

Jump rings have many uses in jewelry making, and although they can be purchased, they can be made very easily and at considerable savings.

The size and strength of a jump ring is determined by the size of the winding

Fig. 8.1 Required length of wire is cut off and straightened by
being placed in vise jaws and pulled with draw tongs.

Fig. 8.2 Winding shank of desired size is selected and wire is wound into tight coil around it.

shank and the gauge of wire used. The wire is first annealed and then straightened by placing one end in a vise and pulling the other end with draw tongs.

Old drill bits are excellent winding shanks. Grip one end of the wire against the winding shank with a pair of pliers and wind the wire into a coil around the shank. Each complete turn will make a jump ring. Remove the wire from the shank and put a saw blade through the coil. Attach the saw blade (preferably a 2/0 gauge blade) and cut carefully through the coil. Craftsmen generally make more than they need so that they may save them for future use.

Fig. 8.3 Saw blade is placed through core of coil and sawed gently into rings.

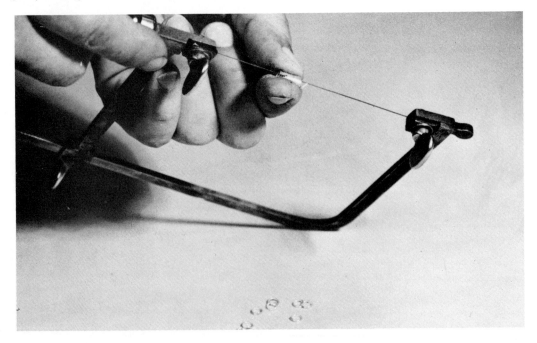

# 9 Forging

The regular thickness of silver wire can become very monotonous. Forging the wire so that it moves from thick to thin and back to thick again adds a sculptural quality and richness to the appearance of the wire. Thus the monotony is replaced by an interest that keeps the eye moving around the design like the current in a stream.

Fig. 9.1 An accurate full-size drawing of the piece is made to serve as a guide in the forging and bending.

Fig. 9.2 The shape of the large curve is formed over a breakhorn stake with a planishing hammer.

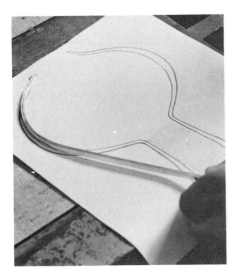

Fig. 9.4 Forging begins at the end of the wire with the convex face of the planishing hammer over the beakhorn.

Fig. 9.3 The shape of the large curve is checked against the drawing for accuracy.

An accurate drawing of the design to scale is necessary, because it becomes the guide for the bending and shaping of the wire. The demonstration piece is forged from 4-mm-square wire. The first curve is shaped around a beakhorn with a planishing hammer. The wire is then laid on the drawing to establish the accuracy of the curve. Begin the forging at the end of the wire by striking the wire with the flat face of the planishing hammer against the beakhorn. The wire should not be forged to more than twice the width of the original thickness of the wire. Therefore, 4-mm wire may be flattened to 8 mm wide. It is not practical to try to achieve this in a single forging however, because the forging

Fig. 9.6 Work-hardened metal is annealed before forging continues.

Fig. 9.5 Forging is continued on a flat surface plate as the curve of the neckpiece changes dimension from square to flat.

38

Fig. 9.7 The metal is also pickled before forging continues.

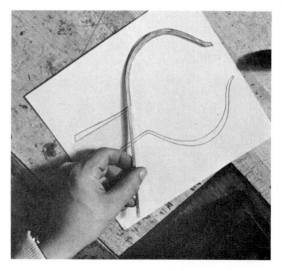

Fig. 9.8 Curve is checked against drawing and marked for bending.

compresses the molecules of the silver and tempers the metal, making it difficult to achieve maximum width. The wire should be annealed periodically to relax the molecules, thus making the metal malleable once more. The demonstration piece was annealed four times. Heavier wire will require several more annealings, and some of the thinner gauges of wire may require none.

The flat curve is forged against a heavy anvil or surface plate with the curved face of the planishing hammer. If the forging of the flat curve changes the shape of the curve so that it does not match the drawing, it may be corrected in this manner. If the curve becomes closed too tightly, concentrate the blows from the

Fig. 9.9 Bend is made against radius of the edge of a T-stake.

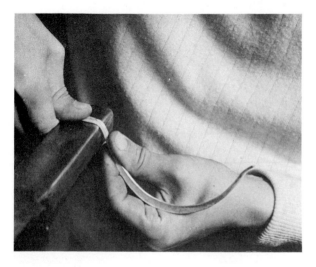

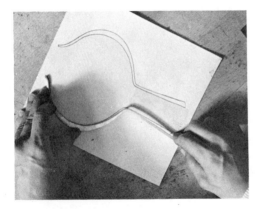

Fig. 9.10 Bend is checked against
drawing for accuracy.

Fig. 9.11 Lower portion of neckpiece
is now forged to flatten and spread wire
to desired width.

hammer on the inside surface of the curve. This will stretch the inside edge and
cause the curve to open. Conversely, if the curve is not closed enough, strike the
wire on the outer surface and this will stretch the outside edge, thus closing the
curve. The forging should be checked against the drawing frequently so that the
shape is maintained throughout the forging. If the shape becomes too distorted,
it will be difficult to correct.

When the curve is completely forged and measured for accuracy against the
drawing, it is marked for bending.

Bending the narrow portions of the wire poses no difficulties. Simply find a
stake with a corresponding curve and bend it to shape. If the metal is annealed,
this can be done by hand and then planished with the planishing hammer.

The piece is then completed by forging the end, marking it for cutting with a
jeweler's saw, filing off the planishing marks, and polishing.

Figs. 9.12, 9.13 Piece is checked against
drawing, marked for cutting and sawed.

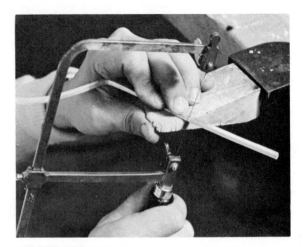

40

# 10 Shaping, Planishing, and Rolling

The play of light on a brightly polished surface is an important consideration in jewelry making. A great deal of life and movement can be added to the metal by giving it a concave, convex, or undulating shape. Such forms can be achieved by first annealing the metal and forcing it down into a concavity, generally carved in a hard wood block or a tree stump. Because the play of light on the surface becomes an integral part of the design, it must be controlled so that it will work well with the design. For this reason, the first shaping must be refined. This is done by placing the piece over a metal stake with a corresponding curve and striking it with the flat side of a planishing hammer to remove any irregularities that might tend to distort highlights.

The marks left by the planishing hammer are often used decoratively because they leave a texture that gives the metal a scintillating play of light. When a smooth surface is preferred, the planish marks are removed by filing over and around the contours of the shape. The piece is then finished with emery cloth and buffing.

The rolling mill should never be used to roll anything other than nonferrous metals such as gold, silver, copper, brass, or bronze. The harder ferrous metals will damage the rollers and the damage will leave an impression on the softer metals. Dirt and dust will also leave an imprint on metal, so the rollers should be thoroughly cleaned.

**Shaping,
Planishing,
and Rolling**

Fig. 10.1 The preliminary shape is forced into the piece by being placed in a crimping stake and struck with a wooden dowel and leather mallet.

Fig. 10.2 Shape is refined over an appropriate stake with flat face of planishing hammer.

Fig. 10.3 Surface irregularities are removed with a flat or hand file.

Fig. 10.4 Concave surface is filed with half-round file to remove irregularities.

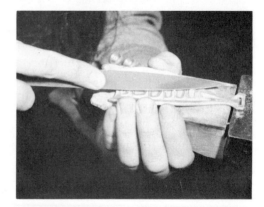

Figs. 10.5, 10.6 Shaping is begun by forcing piece into concave area curved into hardwood block with a wooden mallet.

Heavier gauges of metal can be reduced in thickness with a rolling mill. This will cause the metal to warp as well as become tempered. To compensate for this the metal must be annealed and flattened with a rawhide mallet over a surface plate. Wire can also be flattened. It too may have to be annealed and straightened by stretching, as described in the chapter on Jump Rings (see Fig. 8.1).

A more creative use of this tool can be realized by placing a feather or piece of material such as lace between two pieces of metal and running it through the mill under pressure. This will result in an impression remaining on the surfaces of the metal. The textured metal is then used decoratively.

Fig. 10.7 Shape is refined over appropriate mushroom stake with flat face of planishing hammer.

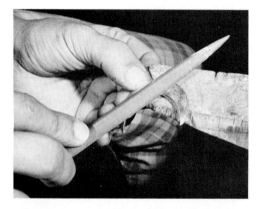 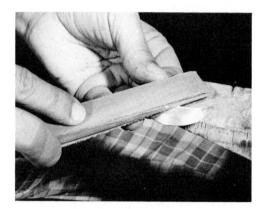

Figs. 10.8, 10.9  Surface irregularities are filed and emeried smooth.

Fig. 10.10  The wire is fed through a rolling mill to make it thinner or flatter.

Fig. 10.11  Tension must be kept on the wire as it is rolled through the mill in order to keep it straight.

# 11 Disc Cutting and Dapping

A circle can be cut from a sheet of silver with a jeweler's saw, but when many circles are needed for a particular design the disc cutter is a very useful tool. It can be purchased to cut discs ranging from 1/8 to 1 inch in diameter.

First place the metal in the slot, then the desired size disc cutter in the corresponding hole and strike it firmly with a heavy hammer.

These discs can be given a three-dimensional quality with the use of a dapping die and dapping punches.

Figs. 11.1, 11.2 Strip of metal is inserted in disc cutter slot under desired size hole. Proper die is inserted in hole and struck soundly with a heavy forging hammer.

Place the disc in the largest concavity and force it down, using a large dapping stake made from a wooden file handle or any similar rounded form and forging hammer. Repeat the procedure in progressively smaller concavities with the metal dapping punches of the proper size for each concavity until the desired shape is reached. It may be necessary to anneal the metal after every third or fourth dapping.

Figs. 11.3, 11.4 Annealed disc is placed in largest concavity in dapping die and struck with a wooden convex shape made from end of file handle.

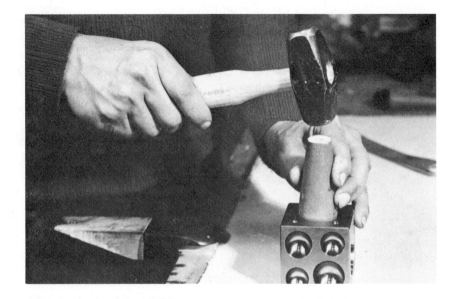

Figs. 11.5, 11.6  Shape is successively refined in smaller concavities with metal dapping punches until desired size and depth are reached.  The size of the dapping punch should fit the concavity of the die allowing for the thickness of the metal.

# 12 Enameling

The appearance of jewelry can be significantly enhanced by the addition of enameling—decorating the surface of metal in one of the oldest ways known to man. Enamel is actually glass, a silica material with metal oxides as a colorant, which fuses to gold, silver, or copper at a temperature of approximately 1500°F and forms a permanent glassy-surfaced bond to the metal. Although enamels and methods of application have been developed for use on steel, aluminum, various other metals, and glass, for purposes of this book and jewelry making we shall consider only those used with the traditional jewelry metals of gold, silver, and copper.

Enamel is available in lump and ground powder form and both types are valuable to the craftsman. Ground enamel is usually purchased from the manufacturer ground to 80 mesh and is sifted with a 60-mesh screen. Lump enamel comes in random lumps ranging from the size of a pea to very small chips, and may be ground in a porcelain or agate mortar to any desired fineness.

Cleanliness is a tremendously important factor in working with enamel. The studio or workspace should be as clean and dust-free as possible, because metal filings, polishing grime, fire scale scrap, and even dust in the air will contaminate the enamel and result in tiny black spots in the finished piece. Each enamel color should be handled and used separately also, to prevent contamination of one color with another.

In designing, whenever possible, the enameled section of the object should be planned for a mechanical attachment to the piece (bezel, prong setting, screwing, riveting, etc.) so that in the event of breakage or chipping of the enamel, it may be removed, repaired, and replaced without destroying the entire piece. No direct silver soldering may be done on a piece once the enamel has been attached because the temperature required for the soldering operation would destroy the enameling.

The following general information regarding preparation of the metal and enamels is applicable to the three techniques described as well as to all the other enameling techniques the craftsman may wish to explore.

The first step in the enameling is the preparation of the metal. It must be clean and completely dust- and oil-free. Lea buffing compound (a water base abrasive) is very satisfactory, or the piece may be cleaned with 320 emery or fine steel wool, but if this is used the cleaning operation should be done in another room or a distant part of the studio and all dust and steel-wool particles carefully removed from the metal before bringing it to the enameling area. Be careful not to touch the cleaned metal surface with fingers. Hold the piece by the edges. The very best metals for enameling are 18K nontarnishing gold, fine silver, or copper. When working with sterling silver it is very important to put a fire skin on the piece before beginning to enamel. This is done by annealing and pickling the sterling three times to build up the fine silver surface as described on page 30). Otherwise, the copper in the sterling alloy will oxidize black each time the piece is fired and in the expansion and contraction of heating and cooling this oxidation (fire scale) will chip off and fly into the enamel, leaving black specks all over the piece. In working with copper, this fire scale cannot be avoided, so the jeweler must be very sure to clean the edges of the piece, removing the fire scale with an abrasive stone (carborundum or scotch stone) under running water after each firing and before the application of the next coat of enamel.

Enamel exerts a tremendous surface tension on the metal. In order to prevent undue warping of the metal and the risk of heavy applications of enamel flaking off, it is important to counter-enamel whenever possible and particularly on metal less than 18 gauge in thickness. Counter-enameling is done first and is merely a coat of enamel fired on the back side of the piece to equalize the surface pull of the enamel on the front.

Enamel is available in both transparent and opaque colors. The preparation of the enamel is essentially the same for both. It must be washed to remove the fine powder residue left by the grinding process which might otherwise create a cloudy effect, distorting the color of the finished piece. Wash no more enamel at one time than can be used in one work session. It is better to wash the enamels several times as more is needed than to wash a large quantity and then try to store the washed enamel for later re-use. Place a small amount of the color to be washed in a shallow bowl or mortar and add distilled water, flooding the enamel powder. Swirl the enamel and water gently and the fine powder and any dirt or other impurities will rise to the surface. Pour off the water and repeat this six or eight times or until the water remains perfectly clear and no pale cloud covers the surface of the enamel grains in the bottom of the bowl. If the enamel is to be applied by sifting, it must be dried by being placed in a shallow covered dish (petrie dishes used in laboratory work are excellent for this but you can improvise with a clean, heavy paper container constructed from drawing paper) and put in a warm place, on top of the heated kiln or in a 200°F oven to dry. If the enamel is to be inlaid or wet packed, the drying process is eliminated and the enamel is ready to use.

In order to facilitate the adherence of the enamel grains to the cleaned metal surface, it is advisable to use a substance that will act as a gum or adhesive. In the past a dilute solution of gum tragacanth was used for this purpose, but there is currently available a synthetic product called Klyr-Fire which burns out completely at a low temperature and leaves no residue that could distort color, particularly in pale transparent enamels. The Klyr-Fire may be applied by brush or by spraying, preferably with a fine nasal atomizer. For large surfaces, when enamel is to be sifted, the spray application is better. The piece is sprayed and the washed and dried enamel in a copper or brass 60 mesh screen sifter is gently sifted on the entire surface of the piece, the piece and the angle of sifting being moved frequently to assure a complete and even coat. The piece is then placed on a trivet or firing rack and put on top of the kiln to dry thoroughly before firing. If the Klyr-Fire is not completely dry when the piece is placed in the hot kiln, the moisture will boil and bubble up instantly, dislodging the enamel grains and leaving pinholes and black spots in the enamel.

The other major method of applying enamel is wet packing or inlaying, and is used in cloisonné and champlevé.

The washed enamel is applied to the prepared metal surface with a fine sable brush or a small spatula which may be purchased or forged from a 3-inch length of 16- to 14-gauge silver wire. The wet enamel is picked up with the brush tip or spatula and placed in position on the metal. It may be pushed into place but does not flow from the brush like pigment. A clean, almost dry brush may be used to clean and straighten color area edges and pick up stray grains of enamel. This is particularly important in cloisonné and champlevé where adjacent areas must be kept clean and uncontaminated by enamel particles of another color. Within the cloisons or lowered areas of the champlevé the enamel may be further moistened with distilled water and the edge of the piece tapped with a fingernail or small tool to level the enamel surface and smooth it out. The excess moisture is then absorbed with an almost dry brush or tiny scrap of facial tissue and a drop of Klyr-Fire added to cement the enamel in place and insure against being accidentally knocked off or disturbed in subsequent wet packing. When all the colors have been put on, all exposed metal edges, cloisonné wires, etc., are carefully cleaned and the piece is put aside to dry on a trivet or rack.

When the piece is thoroughly dry, the firing rack is picked up with an enameling fork or a long-handled trowel and carefully placed in the heated kiln. The kiln pyrometer should read between 1500° and 1650°F. If your kiln does *not* have a pyrometer, test it with pyrometric cones to familiarize yourself with the color of the kiln interior at the proper heat—cone 014 to cone 011 (1540° to 1641°F). The actual firing time should be from one to two minutes, depending on the heat loss from opening the kiln door and the amount of heat absorption of the trivet, rack, and enameled piece. Check the firing progress after 30 to 45 seconds and every 10 seconds thereafter to prevent overfiring and burning of the piece or melting of the metal. This is particularly important in firing cloisonné or any small piece. Obviously large pieces and heavy-gauge metals will require longer firing, because it is the temperature of the metal on which the enamel is placed that causes the enamel flow and fusion to the metal. An underfired piece can always be returned to the kiln for additional firing, but an overfired piece is very difficult to deal with.

If a piece is to be fired many times, the early firings can be underfired as a safety factor because the enamel reflows each time it encounters the heat and the final firings will fully mature it. For counter-enameling and the initial firing of a base coat in cloisonné, the first firing should be to an orangepeel texture rather than the smooth, glassy surface of the final firing.

After the final firing, the piece is allowed to cool slowly and the edges are finished by cleaning under running water with a carborundum stone to remove the fire scale and whatever finish polishing is necessary to bring the edge surfaces to the same finish as the rest of the piece. Specific instructions for various methods of enamel surface finishing are discussed in the following sections on specific techniques.

# CLOISONNÉ

Cloisonné is the oldest known enameling technique, dating back to the early dynastic period in Egypt. It is done with fine wires which are bent to form cloisons or enclosures that contain areas of color.

The design is first drawn carefully and to exact size and a tracing made of it. One copy of the drawing is covered with double-faced transparent tape and the other used as a guide against which the wires are bent to form the cloisons. Cloisonné wire is made from fine silver or fine gold; it is drawn to a very thin flat wire (approximately .010 by .040 inch) and used on edge. Because it must stand on its edge, straight lines are impossible to use unless they are combined with curves or angles to allow the wire to stand up. As each cloison is bent according to the drawing, it is picked up with a fine tweezers and set in place on the tape-covered drawing. This prevents the small wires from being lost or misshapen

Fig. 12.1  Cloisonné wire is bent with fine chain-nose pliers to shapes in drawing.

Fig. 12.2  Bent wire is placed on second drawing covered with double-faced tape.

**52**

**Enameling**

before being fired into the enamel. When all the cloisons have been formed, the metal is prepared for enameling as described in the introduction to enameling.

The prepared metal is painted with a thin coat of Klyr-Fire only on the area to be enameled. A thin base-coat of washed enamel, usually clear flux or white, is sifted on the piece. All excess enamel is blown or carefully brushed from the areas not coated with Klyr-Fire and the piece is set on a firing rack, thoroughly dried, and fired to an orangepeel texture. When the piece has been thoroughly

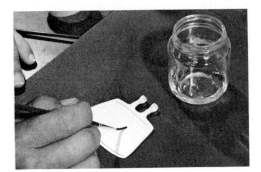

Fig. 12.3  Piece to be enameled is painted lightly with full-strength Klyr-Fire.

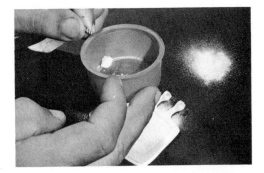

Fig. 12.4  Base-coat of enamel is sifted over entire piece.

Fig. 12.5  Excess enamel is cleaned from exposed metal surfaces of piece with sable brush.

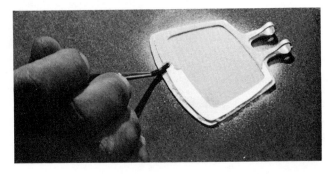

Fig. 12.6  Surplus enamel is immediately returned to jar.

Fig. 12.7  Piece on rack has been fired for the first time to orangepeel texture.

Constructed cloisonné with silver
pendant with chain.
*Charles Swanson*

Cloisonné and silver necklace.
*Jean Delius*

Cast silver ring.
*Jean Delius*

Plique-à-jour and 14K gold ring.
*Dominic DiPasquale*

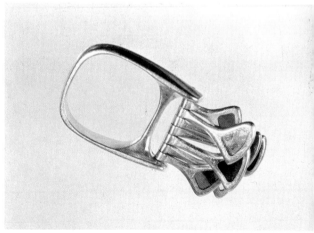

Gold and ebony pendant.
*Jean Delius*

Cloisonné and silver ring.
*Jean Delius*

Cast sterling silver belt buckle.
*Kim Franceschini*

Cloisonné and silver ring.
*Remo Anderson*

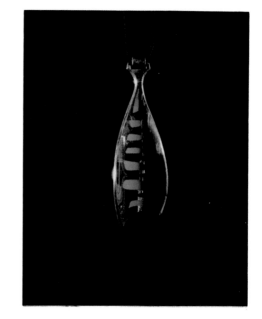

Cast gold pin.
*Jean Delius*

Champlevé and silver pendant.
*Dominic DiPasquale*

Cast gold wedding rings.
*Jean Delius*

Pierced silver pendant with blue stone.
*Mary Tassel*

Cast 14K gold circus rings.
*Mary Ann Spavins*

Constructed silver neck piece
with agate.
*Chris Scharf*

Cast gold and emerald wedding rings.
*Jean Delius*

Cast 14K yellow gold ring
with topaz quartz.
*Darlene Benzon*

Plique-à-jour and silver hair
ornament.
*Dominic DiPasquale*

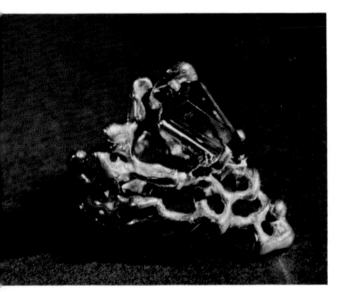

cooled, the cloisons are carefully lifted from the taped drawing with fine tweezers, dipped in full-strength Klyr-Fire, and placed in position on the fired enamel surface. When the Klyr-Fire is thoroughly dry (in 10 to 15 minutes) the piece is placed on a firing rack in the kiln and fired until the enamel is smooth and glassy and the wires have sunk into the enamel. Be careful not to overfire, because the cloisons will melt and disappear. Remember, it is always safer to take the piece out of the kiln to examine it and replace it if it is underfired than to accidently overfire it and have to start all over from the beginning. As soon as the fired piece is removed from the kiln, a flat clean spatula may be used to press gently down on top of the cloisons to assure that they are all sunk equally into the soft enamel, but this must be done very quickly, because the enamel will be hardened in about 5 seconds.

When the piece is thoroughly cooled, you are ready to start wet packing or inlaying the washed enamel colors into the cloisons as described in the introduc-

Figs. 12.8, 12.9   Lower edge of cloisons are dipped in full-strength Klyr-Fire and placed in position on fired enamel and allowed to dry thoroughly before firing.

Fig. 12.10   Immediately after removing piece from kiln, cloisons are pressed firmly down into still soft enamel with a clean, flat spatula.

Fig. 12.11   Prepared wet enamel is packed into cloisons with small spatula.

tory section. It is always preferable to enamel in three or four thin layers, firing each one, than to try to fill the cloisons with one or two thick coats. Greater clarity of color results from a number of thin coats. There are two different effects that may be achieved in cloisonne enamels. Traditionally the cloisons are filled until the fired enamel is flush with the top of the wires. The surface is then ground smooth with a carborundum stone under running water until the wires and enamel are absolutely even when a finger is passed over the surface of the piece. It is then either flash-fired quickly by being returned to a hot kiln just long enough to fire the surface smooth and glassy, or it may be polished by hand, the surface ground with a scotch stone and then 400 wet or dry paper, always under running water. Each succeeding grinding with a finer abrasive replaces deep scratches on the enamel surface with successively finer ones until the final polishing with a felt buff and a paste of cerium oxide restores the shiny surface of the enamel. Hand polishing leaves the enamel with a soft, lustrous surface rather than the very glassy shine of the flash-fired piece. The method used is one of personal preference.

The second method of firing cloisonné is to not completely fill the cloisons, but rather to leave the wires standing above the enamel surface. In the first firing the enamel always adheres to the sides of the wires and the bottom of the cloison, creating a fillet around the edge. Usually one or two firings are enough to achieve this effect. The tops of the wires are then carefully ground to just above the surface of the enamel without scratching the enamel. The metal surfaces are then cleaned and polished and the piece is completed. This second method is the one used in the demonstration piece.

Fig. 12.12 Piece is tapped lightly on edge to level wet enamel in cloisons, and is then thoroughly dried and fired as before.

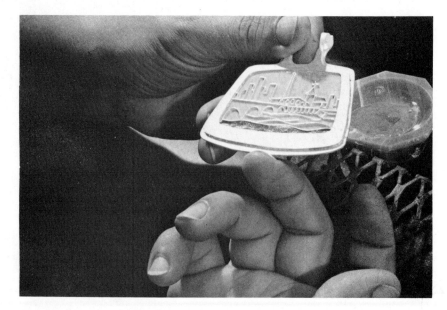

## CHAMPLEVÉ

Champlevé (literally, *raised field*) is the second oldest of the enameling techniques, with its earliest forms dating from the Eighteenth Dynasty (1567-1320 B.C.) in Egypt. In champlevé, portions of the metal are lowered and filled with enamel so that the finished surface is part polished metal, part enamel, and perfectly smooth.

In contemporary work, preparation of the metal may be done in either of two ways. In the first and more traditional approach, a heavy piece of metal, usually 16-gauge or thicker, is coated with a ground or resist. The design to be enameled is then scratched through the ground with an etching stylus and the metal thus exposed is etched away in a nitric acid bath (see section on etching, p. 68), until depressions about 1/32-inch deep are created to hold the enamel. The ground is then removed and the piece cleaned and fire-coated before enameling.

The second method, the one used in the demonstration piece, is done by piercing the design to be enameled from a piece of 20-gauge metal and then sweat soldering it (see p. 24) to a sheet of 18-gauge metal. The lowered areas thus created are then filled with enamel.

The metal is prepared as described in the enameling introduction and the piece is then carefully wet packed or inlaid with the prepared enamel colors. Be sure to carefully clean any stray grains of enamel from the surfaces and edges of the piece and dry thoroughly before firing. As in cloisonné, it is better to fill and fire three or four times than to try to save time by putting too much enamel on at once. The final enamel firing should bring the enamel surface slightly above the exposed metal surface so that both surfaces may be ground absolutely flush with no depressions in the enamel. Again, the grinding is done under running water with a flat or curved carborundum stone, depending on whether the surface of the piece is flat or concave as in the demonstration piece. When the entire surface of the metal and enamel is perfectly smooth, the deep scratches are removed with scotch stone and 400 wet or dry paper under running water and then the surface is polished with a felt buff and a paste of cerium oxide to bring it to the desired luster. If, in the grinding process, small pits or pinholes appear in the enamel, these must be filled with new enamel, refired, and reground. After grinding and before polishing it is wise to be sure that all carborundum is removed from the enamel surface by cleaning thoroughly with a fiberglass brush.

Figs. 12.13, 12.14  The opaque enamel is ground in agate mortar with distilled water and drained. Washing and draining is repeated as many times as necessary until all fine dust and impurities are removed and water remains unclouded.

Fig. 12.15  Wet enamel is inlaid in recessed areas of piece with small spatula.

Fig. 12.16  Excess enamel grains are removed from surface of piece with a damp fine red sable brush.

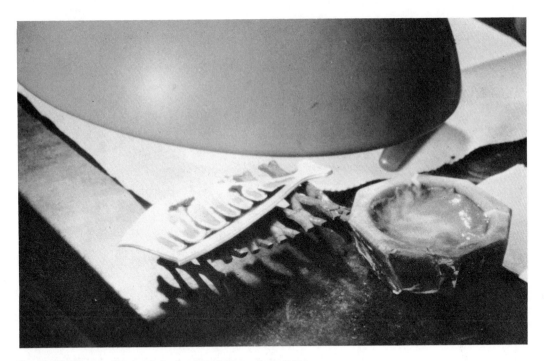

Fig. 12.17   Piece on firing rack is placed under incandescent lamp
(or on top of heated kiln) to dry enamel thoroughly before firing.

Fig. 12.18   Piece on rack is placed in
heated kiln (1500° to 1600°F).

Fig. 12.19   After recessed areas are filled
level or above surface, piece is ground
under water with carborundum stone,
followed by scotch stone and polishing.

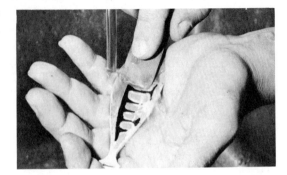

## PLIQUE à JOUR

Plique à jour (*light of day*) enamel is a technique resembling the stained glass technique, because there is no metal backing behind the enamel. This is the most fragile of all enamel techniques and obviously should be used only in a design which, when worn, permits light to pass through the enameled areas to show them to the greatest advantage. Drop earrings are an excellent problem in plique à jour. The demonstration piece, an ornamental hairpin, when worn allows the light to shine through the transparent enamel shapes. Pins, pendants, and rings are generally *not* practical uses for this technique because the body prevents the transmittal of light.

In designing for plique à jour, the pierced areas should not be more than 1/4 square inch in area because unsupported enamel in larger areas tends to fracture too easily. When the metal has been pierced and filed, prepare it for enameling as described in the enameling introduction. Place the prepared metal on a clean sheet of mica on a firing rack. Mica is used as a backing in plique à jour enameling because the enamel does not adhere to the mica, but only to the metal edges of the pierced areas. The enamel used in this technique is in lump, *not* ground, form and is always transparent. Use a clean sheet of white paper for each color in the design. Pour a quantity of enamel lumps on the paper and with fine jeweler's tweezers pick out very small lumps and carefully place them in the appropriate pierced areas. Pack them as close together as possible and mound them slightly above the surface of the metal, being careful not to allow any to

58

fall on the metal surfaces. It is important to be very careful in moving the piece on its firing rack and mica from the work space to the kiln. The lump enamel is much more easily distrubed than the ground and inlaid enamel. If any lumps are knocked out of place, they must be replaced before the piece is put into the kiln. Allow to cool after firing and fill any holes or spaces that appear; refire until each pierced area is totally filled and the enamel mounded slightly above the surface of the metal. After the piece has thoroughly cooled, remove it from the mica and, very carefully holding it against a flat surface to support it (a small piece of 1/4-inch wood stripping or masonite works well for this), grind it under running water with a carborundum stone on both front and back until all surfaces of metal and enamel are flush. This must be done with great care and

Fig. 12.20   Pierced piece of silver is fire-skinned.

Fig. 12.21   Piece is placed on sheet of mica on firing rack and enamel lumps are carefully inserted in pierced holes.

Fig. 12.23   Piece is inspected during firing. At this point enamel lumps are just starting to flow and fill pierced areas.

Fig. 12.22   Filled piece on rack is carefully placed in hot kiln.

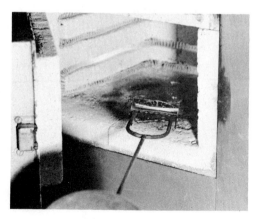

gentleness in order not to fracture the unsupported enamel. It is then advisable to finish by hand polishing as described in cloisonné and champlevé to return the enamel surfaces to their true luster and transparency. It is possible to flash-fire to regain the transparency, but the grinding of the enamel and metal surfaces removes the fire coat on the metal so that when it is placed in the kiln for the flash-firing it will oxidize black and the craftsman is faced with the problem of removing this oxidation without scratching the enamel. This flash-fire method of finishing is practical only when working on fine silver or fine gold which will not oxidize. Always remember that the finished piece is much more fragile than other types of enamel and must be handled with great care.

Fig. 12.24 After several fillings and firings when all pierced areas are completely filled, piece is allowed to cool and is ground under water with carborundum stone on both sides so that enamel and metal surfaces are absolutely flush and no enamel is left on exposed metal.

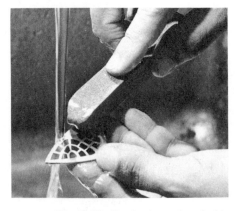

Fig. 12.25 Stoning is continued with finer scotch stone.

Fig. 12.26 Cerium oxide, moistened with water to a paste, is applied to wet felt ring buff.

Fig. 12.27 Piece is kept moist with wet cerium oxide and buffed to desired finish.

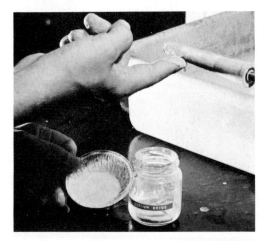

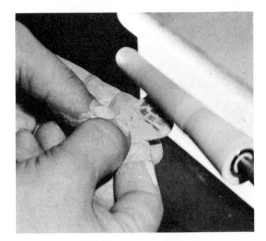

# 13 Reticulation

Unlike etching and repousse, which are controlled methods of enriching a surface, reticulation is less certain in terms of the results but it is often extremely effective and exciting.

For reticulation the preferred alloy is 82 parts fine silver to 18 parts copper. However, it is possible to use sterling for this process. Start with a piece of 22-gauge sheet somewhat larger than the object you wish to make. Place it in an annealing pan and anneal it following the instructions on page 30. After remov-

Fig. 13.1 Silver is laid in annealing pan and heated with soft flame as per instructions in section on annealing (pp 30-31).

Fig. 13.2 Silver is immersed in heated pickle solution.

ing it from the pickle solution, brush it with soapy water solution and a brass wire brush. Repeat this five times. Anneal it once more so the haze appears on the metal and immerse it in the pickle for several moments but do not brass wire brush it with soapy water.

The purpose of this procedure is to build up a fine silver skin on the surface of the metal. Because the melting point of sterling is lower than that of fine silver, the sterling that is sandwiched between the fine silver skin will melt first, causing the surface metal to wrinkle or reticulate when it reaches the melting point of sterling.

Fig. 13.3 Silver is brushed with soapy water and fine brass brush.

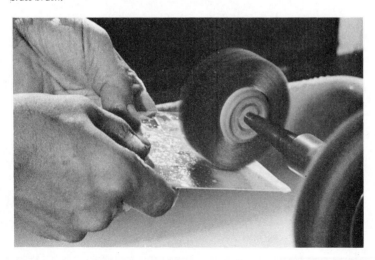

Fig. 13.4 Tip of hot flame is used to reticulate prepared silver.

Place the piece of metal on an asbestos pad and heat the piece generally with the torch. Increase the air to achieve a hotter flame and apply the tip of the flame to the metal. As it begins to reticulate, move the torch until the entire piece is finished. The difference in melting points of sterling and fine silver is very little, so caution must be used in order to prevent the entire piece from melting.

Fig. 13.5 Selected section to be used in finished piece has been sawed from reticulated sheet.

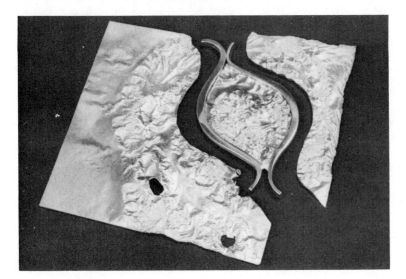

# 14 Fusing

Jewelers invariably accumulate numerous pieces of scrap silver from cutting designs. These scraps may be used for casting, but silver lends itself very well to a process that is called fusing. It is an uncomplicated yet potentially very creative way of making some extremely exciting pieces of jewelry.

Fusing silver is accomplished by heating the silver to the point at which the surface of the metal becomes molten, allowing the molecules of the separate pieces to interpenetrate and become one piece. No solder is used.

There are a number of ways to approach fusing. One effective way is to fuse the scraps to a piece of 22-gauge sheet silver. This adds strength and provides a smoother back that can be polished and will not catch on clothing.

The sheet of silver must be paste-fluxed and the pieces placed in position on the sheet and sprinkled with borax powder or liquid flux. Then heat the piece gently to allow the flux to flow and prevent the oxidation of the metal. If the boiling action of the flux causes the pieces to move, they may be pushed back into position with a soldering pick. When the flux reaches a fluid state, intensify the heat on small areas, bringing the surfaces to a molten state. The more molten the surface becomes, the more reticulation you will achieve. Too much heat may result in the total melting of the pieces and the loss of any of the intended design characteristics. Continue the fusing until you have achieved the desired effect. When completed, immerse in the pickle solution.

Fig. 14.1  A bottom piece of 22-gauge silver is coated with paste flux.

Fig. 14.2  Small pieces of silver scrap and wire are arranged in a pleasing design on the fluxed silver surface.

Fig. 14.3  Powdered borax is sprinkled lightly over the piece.

Fig. 14.4  A soft flame gently heats total piece until flux becomes fluid.

Figs. 14.5, 14.6  A more intense and direct flame (more oxygen added to gas) is concentrated on each area, bringing the surfaces to the degree of fusion and reticulation that is desired.

Finish the piece by cutting away the exterior portions of the bottom sheet and piercing areas to accent the design. Polish with buffers and oxidize the lower areas if desired.

Figs. 14.7, 14.8 After the excess 22-gauge sheet from the outer edges of the piece have been sawed away, negative areas within the design are accented by piercing.

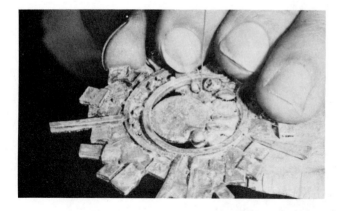

Fig. 14.9 Rough edges are now filed and design is refined.

Wire can also be fused together with careful control of the heat application. After applying the flux, heat the wire generally and then concentrate a small sharp flame directly to the areas that are touching and remove the heat as soon as fusing occurs.

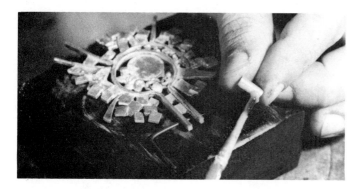

Figs. 14.10, 14.11, 14.12 A small piece of silver tubing is soldered to the top of the piece and filed to a perfect fit. This will serve as a hanger through which a cord or chain may be strung to make a pendant.

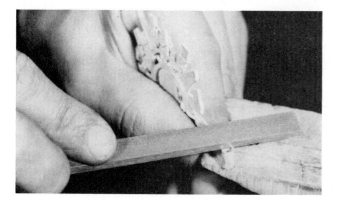

# 15 Etching

Surface embellishment may take many forms in jewelry making. One of the most effective ways of enriching a surface is by etching a design into the metal much the same as a graphic artist etches a copper plate. This approach is particularly useful to people who like to draw. The example piece shown is pictorial. Jewelers more frequently use this technique decoratively, but in either case it can be most effective.

After contructing the piece of jewelry, polish it to remove all scratches from the surface. This final polishing is done prior to the etching, because any polishing after the piece is etched may break down the crispness of the etched edges and distort the image.

There are a number of etching grounds commercially available. Most hard grounds seem to work well. Paint the etching ground over the entire piece, paying particular attention to the edges. Coat it a second time both front and back if necessary. Allow to dry thoroughly.

Draw through the etching ground with a stylus. Any area or line that is drawn will expose the metal and will be etched by the acid.

When the drawing or decoration is complete, immerse the piece in a solution of one part nitric acid to two parts water. This is a strong solution and will work fairly quickly. Some craftsmen prefer one part acid to three or four parts water.

Fig. 15.1 Ground is applied to completed pendant.

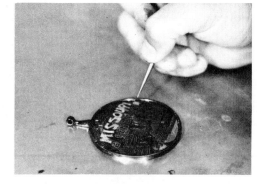

Figs. 15.2, 15.3 Design is drawn through ground with stylus.

Fig. 15.4 Measured acid is poured gently into water.

Fig. 15.5  Pendant is immersed in acid solution.

*It is extremely important to add the acid to the water* when mixing this solution, because adding water to acid causes a violent reaction. The mixture should also be used in a well-ventilated area.

Small bubbles will form over the areas of exposed metal. They should be whisked away with a brush or feather or they will interfere with the etching.

Fig. 15.6  Bubbles formed by etching solution are gently brushed from surface of pendant.

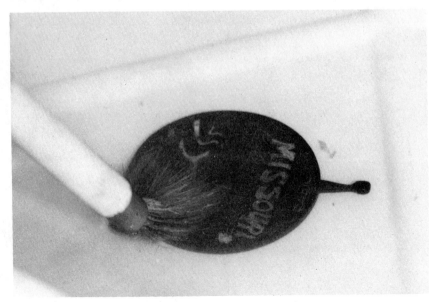

Fig. 15.7 Flaked or disturbed ground is retouched as necessary.

The etching process will take from ten to fifteen minutes with this acid strength, depending on the desired depth of cut.

If, during the etching, some of the ground should flake off, remove the piece from the acid, rinse and dry it off, and recoat the areas where flaking has occurred. When the ground dries, continue with the etching.

Fig. 15.8 Solvent is poured over piece to dissolve ground.

When the etching is completed, clean the piece by pouring recommended solvent over it and rubbing it with sawdust or cheese cloth.

Finish the piece by oxidizing the recessed areas to accent the design.

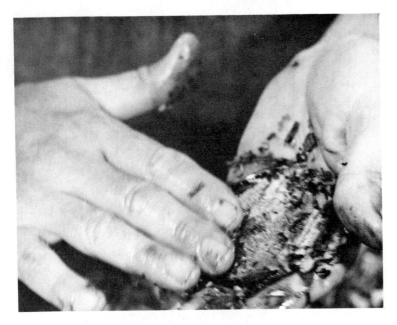

Figs. 15.9, 15.10  Dissolved ground is completely removed from pendant with sawdust and clean towel.

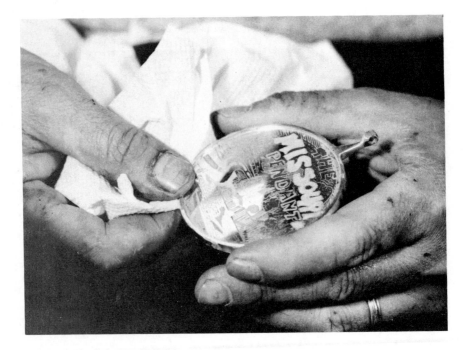

# 16 Stone Setting

Stones can be set in jewelry with prongs or bezels. The method used depends largely on the stone. Faceted stones are usually set with prongs, while cabochons and other unfaceted stones are set with bezel settings.

## PRONG SETTINGS

Prong settings are available from jewelry supply outlets in all shapes and sizes. Many craftsmen, however, prefer to make their own. The following demonstration provides a simple and handsome approach to making a prong setting.

The wire used is 18-gauge round and is bent into a U-shape around the end of a pair of round-nose pliers. Each U-shape is made about 1/2-inch long. If four prongs are desired, four U-shapes are used. If six prongs are desired, six U-shapes are used, etc.

After all the shapes are uniformly bent, they are laid on a flat charcoal block so that the sides touch and the bottoms are evenly lined up. This is accomplished

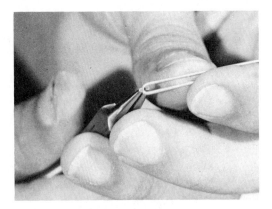

Fig. 16.1 Round wire is bent into U-sahpe with round-nose pliers.

Fig. 16.2 U-shaped wires are laid tangent to straight edge and fluxed.

by placing a straight edge at the bottom of the shapes, and lining them up so the bottom of the U is tangent to the straight edge. The vertical lines of the U's should be perfectly perpendicular to the straight edge. Flux the wires where they touch and heat the flux until it becomes fluid. If the wires move during the heating, push them back in place with a soldering pick. Place a solder pellet on

Fig. 16.3 Solder pellets are applied to wire joints.

the joint of the wires and solder the wires together. Place the piece in the pickle solution for several minutes. Form the piece to the shape of the stone, using round-nose pliers and solder. Then spread the ends of the prongs to form a crown. Place the stone in the setting and measure and cut the length of the

Fig. 16.4 Wires are soldered together.

Figs. 16.5, 16.6 Wires are formed to shape of stone with round-nose pliers and soldered together.

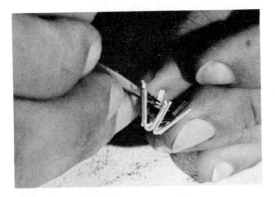

Fig. 16.7 Wires have been spread to form crown. Stone is inserted and prongs are marked for cutting.

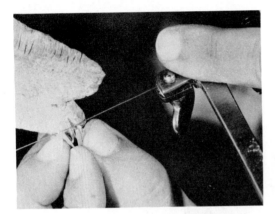

Fig. 16.8 Prongs are sawed to desired length.

prongs. The extension of the prong above the stone will vary depending on the gauge of wire used and the size of the stone. In any case, the prongs should extend enough beyond the stone to be bent over to hold the stone securely without disturbing the appearance of the stone. Solder the setting securely to a base which has already been soldered to the ring. After pickling, place the stone

Fig. 16.9 Crown is soldered to base, which has already been soldered to the ring.

Fig. 16.10 With stone leveled in setting, girdle of stone is marked with scriber carefully on each prong.

Fig. 16.11 A stone-setting burr is used to cut groove in each prong on which stone will seat.

level in the setting and mark the top edge of the girdle with a scriber on the inside of each prong. Then cut grooves into the prongs with a stone-setting burr in a flexible shaft at these marked points. Care must be taken to be certain that these grooves are all cut at the same level to prevent the stone from being tipped in the setting. Use jeweler's saw to split the prongs from the top to the center of

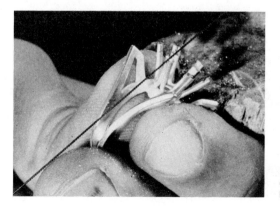

Fig. 16.12 Each double prong end is split along solder line to bottom of groove.

the groove along the soldered line. Then snap the stone in place and bend the prongs over the stone with prong-setting pliers. The ends of the prongs must now be polished to avoid their snagging on material.

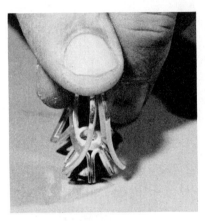

Fig. 16.13 Stone is snapped in place in setting.

Fig. 16.14 Prong-setting pliers are used to tighten prongs against stone.

Fig. 16.15 Prong ends are carefully filed and polished.

## BEZELS

Essentially, a bezel is a strip of thin, flat wire that encompasses a stone and holds it to the piece of jewelry. Bezels are generally used in setting cabachons and other unfaceted stones. They may be round, oval, square, or freeform shapes.

The width of the bezel wire should be compatible to the height of the stone. One-half the height of the stone is a fair rule of thumb but this may be unsatisfactory for very thin or heavy stones.

The bezel wire is bent tightly around the stone and cut with a jeweler's saw where it overlaps. The edges are brought together with tension and soldered with

Fig. 16.16  Flat wire is formed around stone so that seam will be on the long side of stone.

Fig. 16.17  Ends of bezel are brought together under tension and soldered with hard solder.

hard solder. The stone is then placed in the bezel to adjust the shape and check it for size. If it is too small it may be stretched by being placed it on a mandrel and struck lightly with a planishing hammer. The stone must fit the bezel with *no friction* because the bezel will be rigid when soldered to the piece. The bottom of the bezel must be flat so that it fits perfectly to the base to which it is to be soldered. The solder pellets should be placed on the inside of the bezel and the solder drawn out for the neatest joint.

Fig. 16.18 Bezel is shaped to conform exactly with stone, using half-round pliers.

Fig. 16.19 When bezel is too tight it is stretched over mandrel with flat face of planishing hammer.

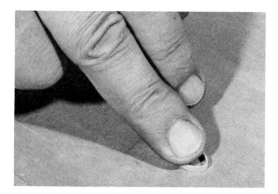

Fig. 16.20 Bottom of bezel is flattened by rubbing on emery cloth.

Fig. 16.21 Bezel is placed in position and solder pellets are placed around inside of bezel.

Fig. 16.22 Bezel is soldered in place, concentrating heat on base piece to bring it to soldering temperature at the same time as the much smaller bezel.

81

Figs. 16.23, 16.24 Engraver's ball is used to securely hold piece as the bezel is chased against the stone with chasing tool and hammer.

The stone is placed in the bezel and the bezel is chased against the stone with a chasing tool and hammer.

When setting a transparent stone with a bezel, most of the area beneath the stone should be pierced away, leaving a seat for the stone to sit on. This allows light to be transmitted through the stone and enhances its appearance significantly. Certain stones, such as moonstones, opals, and star sapphires, will be most effectively displayed if the entire interior of the bezel (sides and solid bottom) are oxidized a deep black before setting the stone.

# 17 Hinging

There are many ways to join bracelet links. The simplest method of accomplishing this is with jump rings. A much richer and more professional look can be achieved by hinging the links together. When the following procedure is used, hinging becomes a relatively simple operation.

The links that are to be hinged together must have straight edges, because it is impossible to hinge around a curve. It is important to file a concave groove in the edge so that the tubing will rest tightly against the edge of the link. This will result in a neater and stronger soldered joint.

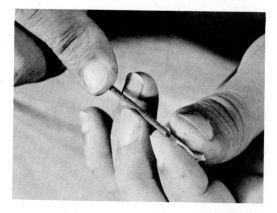

Fig. 17.1 Groove is filed in edge of link to be hinged to fit size of tubing used in hinge.

Begin by dividing the edge of the link to be hinged into three or five equal parts. Five are more desirable than three because there will be less chance for the hinge to loosen up with wear. Transfer the measurement of the divisions to the tube cutting gauge. Select the size tubing that is best proportioned for the design and saw as many cheniers as may be needed. Remove any burrs that may be on each of the cheniers as a result of the sawing.

Place an end of a piece of fine binding wire in a vise. Grasp the other end with a pair of draw tongs and pull it so that it is perfectly straight. Cut two pieces of the binding wire about 1/4-inch longer than the full length of the hinge. Place two of the cheniers on one piece of binding wire and three cheniers on the other. Place the cheniers on a charcoal block in a meshed position. Make certain the edges of the cheniers are touching each other. Place the links in position, preferably bottom side up, so that it will be easier to clean off any excess solder if necessary. Apply the flux sparingly to those areas to be soldered.

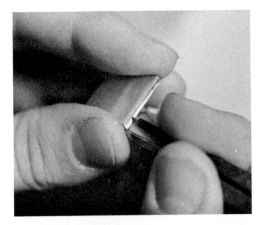

Fig. 17.2 Length of hinge is divided into five equal parts with dividers.

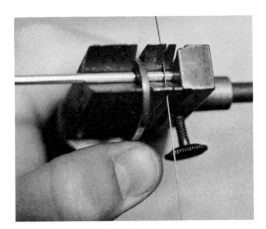

Fig. 17.3 Measurement of each chenier has been set on tube cutting gauge and tubing is placed in gauge and the required number of cheniers are sawed.

Fig. 17.4 Links are placed on charcoal block bottom side up with cheniers on two pieces of binding wire in meshed position.

Fig. 17.5  Flux has been applied to cheniers and links very carefully and heated. Small solder pellets are placed on each seam joint and soldered.

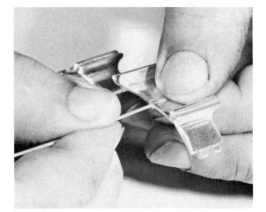

Fig. 17.6  After finishing, links are assembled and rivet wire inserted in each hinge (rivet wire should be a snug fit in cheniers).

Heat the flux so that it becomes sticky. If the boiling action of the flux causes any of the cheniers to move out of position, move them back before applying the solder. The solder pellets should be about half the length of the cheniers. Place them on the joint and proceed with the soldering. When completed, remove the binding wire and place the links in the pickle solution.

When all of the cheniers have been soldered to the links, take a piece of rivet wire that will fit snugly in the chenier holes. File a point on the wire so that it will thread its way through the hinge more easily. Cut the rivet wire off so that a 1/32-inch is exposed on either side of the hinge. Place one end of the hinge against a metal stake and chase the other end with a rivet hammer or chasing tool. Repeat this on the opposite end of the rivet. Bracelet links should be polished before the cheniers are soldered to the links. If polishing is necessary after the cheniers have been attached, the links should be riveted first or the buffing wheel will wear down the edges of the cheniers.

Fig. 17.7  Rivet wire is sawed off leaving approximately 1/64" extending from each end of hinge.

Fig. 17.8  Wire is riveted in place holding hinge section against a flat metal surface by peening ends of wire with small end of chasing hammer or rivet hammer.

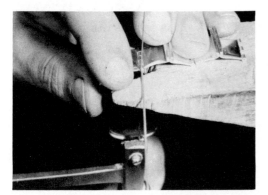

Ring cast from carved model.

Ring cast from built-up model.

# 18 Centrifugal Casting

## MODEL MAKING

The first step in lost wax casting is to prepare the wax model. This may be accomplished in many ways and with a variety of waxes. Experimentation with all the available waxes is encouraged so that one can discover which materials are most suitable to his sense of design and style of work.

### CARVING METHOD

Hard waxes are generally carved with the use of a flexible shaft (p. 17) and burrs, which are available in varying shapes and degrees of coarseness. Equally good results *can* be achieved using a variety of files, engraving tools, knives, or any other tool fashioned to achieve a particular effect.

Fig. 18.1 Block of wax is pierced with tri-cornered scraper.

Fig. 18.2 Opening is enlarged to 1 1/2 size smaller than desired ring size.

Fig. 18.3 Mandrel is heated to melting point of wax.

Fig. 18.4  Wax model is eased up to desired size with twisting motion. To compensate for taper of mandrel, model is reversed and process is repeated.

Fig. 18.6  Inside of ring shank is smoothed with half-round file.

Fig. 18.5  Excess wax is cut away with wax saw blade.

Fig. 18.7  The model is smoothed and equalized.

Figs. 18.8, 18.9  The model is sculptured, using flexible shaft with appropriate burrs and/or files.

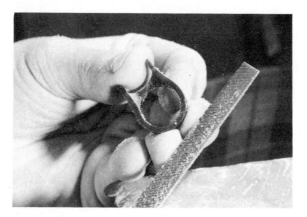

89

**Centrifugal Casting**    The same hard wax may be used in an entirely different manner. That is, instead of carving away the wax to reveal a form, the design is built up by applying hot wax over wax. This may be accomplished using an alcohol lamp and a variety of dental tools. A far more efficient method is to use an electric waxer with a rheostat heat control. There are a number of these tools available with different features; all of them are capable of delivering satisfactory results. After a piece has been built up using this method, it may be further sculptured with the flexible shaft, files, etc., to achieve the desired effect.

Wax is also available in sheet form. It comes in several gauges of thickness as well as degrees of hardness and flexibility and is easily molded, pierced, and textured. The results are therefore quite different from the other discussed.

Fig. 18.10 Cylinder of paper is made to desired ring size, then covered with tracing paper. The wax is picked up with waxing tip.

Fig. 18.11 Wax is deposited over cylinder to build up the design.

Fig. 18.12 Buildup is continued until desired form is achieved.

Wax wire can be purchased in round, square, half-round, and triangular shapes. The waxer or heated dental tools are very effective in joining wax wire. The thinner wires are very flexible and can be used to create extremely delicate and complicated designs.

Microcrystaline waxes, a product of petroleum companies, are completely different from the other waxes. They become soft from handling and are far more plastic than the other waxes used in casting. They can be stretched, pulled, or rolled, and when heated to a fluid state, the wax can be built up by applying wax over wax with a paintbrush, thereby developing a "painted" effect.

Naturally, all of the above waxes may be used in combination to achieve special effects.

Fig. 18.13 (Optional) When more sculptural effect is desired, the model is finished, using appropriate burrs and flexible shaft and/or files.

## SPRUING

When the model is completed, it must be sprued for investing. Generally, a single 10-gauge sprue attached to the shank of a wax ring model is sufficient. However, if the ring model has an undercut, it is important to sprue it up so that the investment flows freely around the entire model without trapping any air. This may require three sprues of 14- or 16-gauge wire and positioning of the model horizontally. Larger pieces such as pins and pendants generally require three sprues of 14- or 12-gauge wax wire.

After the sprues have been attached, weight the model to determine the amount of metal you will need for casting. (Refer to the tables on p. 139.) The model is then ready to be set in the sprue cone, which is made of plasticene and should be large enough to receive the entire volume of metal required for the casting. Make the sprue cone smooth and have it angle up at a full 45 degrees so as to permit a smooth, even flow of the metal into the investment.

If a design is very complicated, with delicate patterns, fine lines, or small depressions, best results can be achieved by double investing the model. This is accomplished by mixing a tablespoon of investment to a smooth creamy consistency, vibrating it to remove air bubbles, and painting the mixture over the model, making certain the investment is pushed into all the crevices. Build this layer up about 1/8-inch thick. This procedure may be bypassed when the model is free of fine detail.

The next step is to place the cottle over the model and seal the base with plasticene so that it will not leak. Commercial cottles are made of stainless steel and are reusable. An excellent substitute for a cottle and one that is far more practical, particularly in a classroom situation, is a simple tin can. The one precaution necessary when using a tin can is to be certain it fits into the cradle of the centrifuge. If the can is too long for the cradle, it can be cut to size with a pair of aviation shears. The cottle or tin can should extend at least 1/4-inch above the sprued model.

Fig. 18.14 Sprue wire is attached to model with waxer.

Fig. 18.15 Model is weighed to determine amount of metal needed for casting.

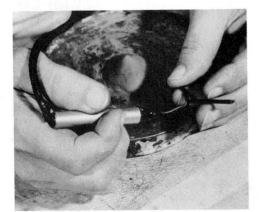

Fig. 18.16 Sprue cone is formed of plasticene on flat metal surface, then a hole is made in plasticene to receive sprue.

Fig. 18.17 Plasticene is pushed around sprue.

Fig. 18.18 Model is painted with debubblizer.

Fig. 18.19 Cottle is placed over model and bottom sealed with plasticene.

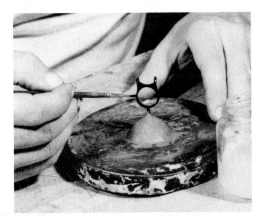

# INVESTING

Heat-resistant plasters are used to invest models. Ordinary household plasters and plaster of Paris will fracture during burnout and are therefore unsatisfactory. One investment plaster in particular, which is gray in color because it contains graphite, delivers a high degree of detail and has the added advantage of turning bone-white in the kiln when it is ready for casting.

The amount of investment used should be 1 1/3 times the volume of the cottle. Place the investment in a rubber bowl, add room-temperature water, and mix to achieve a creamy but fluid consistency. Place the bowl on a vibrator to allow trapped air bubbles to rise. Then place the cottle on the vibrator and pour the investment down the side of the cottle—not directly on the model. This entire process should take no more than three or four minutes.

Allow the investment to cure about two hours before the burnout.

Fig. 18.20 Investment is placed in rubber bowl.

Fig. 18.21 Room-tempeature water is added.

94

Fig. 18.22 Investment is mixed to proper consistency.

Fig. 18.23 Investment is vibrated to remove trapped air bubbles.

Fig. 18.24 Cottle is placed on the vibrator and investment poured down the side of the flask.

Fig. 18.25  Investment is placed in kiln on supports to permit drainage and evaporation of wax, brought to temperature as described in text.

## BURNOUT

Remove the plasticene sprue cone and sealer and place the investment in the kiln with the sprue hole facing down. Place it on a support so that the wax will flow out freely and vaporize. It is important to bring the temperature up slowly and steadily to about 1250° to 1300°F. This should take approximately 2 to 2 1/2 hours. If three or more castings are burned out simultaneously, the burnout time will increase considerably, especially in a small burnout kiln.

## CASTING

When removing the cottle from the kiln, turn it horizontally to avoid the possibility of dropping it. An orange glow in the sprue hole indicates that it is ready for casting. Any black residue around the sprue hole indicates that there is still carbon remaining in the mold and the burnout should continue until it disappears.

Place the investment in the cradle and push the crucible plate up against the face of the investment. The orange glow of the sprue hole should be visible

Centrifugal
Casting

Fig. 18.26  New crucibles must be
entirely fluxed for initial use.

Fig. 18.27  Investment is removed from
kiln in horizontal position.

Fig. 18.28  Investment is placed in
cradle and face plate is pushed up
tight against cottle.

through the face plate. Place the metal in the crucible and balance the arm. (Note: new crucibles must be coated with flux to seal their porosity.) Wind the centrifuge two full turns and set the restraining pin. Cock the arm of the centrifuge. Bring the metal to a molten state. If slag should form on the metal, sprinkle it lightly with borax. When the metal is completely fluid and has the appearance of liquid mercury, release the retraining pin and allow the centrifuge to spin until it stops. Remove the cottle from the cradle and wait until the button (silver in the cone) no longer glows. Plunge it into cold water while the investment is still hot and the plaster will disintegrate. Remove the casting, cut off the sprue, and finish by filing, emerying, and buffing.

Fig. 18.29   Metal is placed in the crucible.

Fig. 18.30   Centrifuge is balanced.

Fig. 18.31   Centrifuge is wound and restraining pin is set.

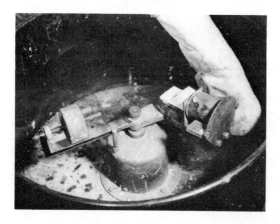

Fig. 18.32   Arm is cocked 90 degrees to the right.

Fig. 18.33   Torch flame is applied to melt metal.

Fig. 18.34  When necessary, borax is added to clean the metal.

Fig. 18.35  Metal is heated until it has mercury appearance.

Fig. 18.36    Restraining pin is released and centrifuge is allowed to
spin.

Fig. 18.37    When metal no longer glows, it is plunged into cold
water.

# 19 Finishing

Sterling silver and gold can be polished to a mirrorlike finish, but there are alternatives that may be more appropriate for some pieces of jewelry. Scratches are much more apparent on high finishes. Rings, because they are worn on fingers which grasp coins, silverware, tools, and many other things, tend to scratch easily, so brightly polished finishes are less desirable than a scratch or brush finish, which tends to conceal scratches acquired in normal use. Pendants, pins, and earrings can be highly polished and remain that way provided care is used in putting them away. Many craftsmen prefer the scratch or brush finish for all kinds of jewelry. Their reason is more aesthetic than practical. Fine silver has a softer, richer, and more lustrous look than sterling silver. The appearance of fine silver can be given to sterling by polishing the finished piece to a high shine, annealing the piece to oxidize the copper on the surface, immersing it in pickle solution to remove this surface copper, and brushing the piece in one direction with a brass wire brush and soapy water solution at 700 to 1000 RPM. This should be repeated three times to achieve a substantial fire skin.

Polishing is a system of replacing scratches and irregularities in the metal with finer scratches until the scratches become invisible to the naked eye. When the scratches and irregularities are severe, it is necessary to begin with files and follow with emery cloth to prepare the piece for buffing. Generally, a number 2 cut file is sufficient for preparing the surface for the emery cloth. Because of the irregularities created by the hammer, the heavy forged wire (figs. 00) is first filed with a number zero file. Flat and convex surfaces are filed with flat files; concave shapes and edges are filed with the round side of a half-round file. A piece of 240-grade emery cloth on an emery stick will remove the file marks. This is followed by 320 emery cloth also used on an emery stick to continue to reduce the scratches. When two pieces of 320 emery paper are thoroughly rubbed together, the coarseness of the paper is significantly reduced and the result is excellent for the final step before buffing or as a finish, should a scratch finish be desired.

Because buffing compounds vary in coarseness, each buffing wheel should be used exclusively with a single compound. The initial compound used may be either diamond white or tripoli on a buffing machine capable of delivering 3500 to 4000 RPM. Both compounds are effective in removing the scratches left by

Fig. 19.1 Surface on which bezel is to be soldered must be finished prior to soldering. It is first filed to remove deepest scratches.

Fig. 19.2 File marks are removed with emery cloth over emery stick.

Fig. 19.3 Buffing wheel for tripoli is about to be charged with that compound.

**104**   the emery cloth. The green compound will bring the metal to a bright mirror finish, and red rouge will add an even greater shine if desired.

Dark spots may appear on the brightly polished surface. They are the result of fire scale and may be removed by additional emerying and polishing. If a high finish is desired, this fire scale should be removed, but if a scratch brush finish is to be put on the piece, the dark spots will disappear with the following process.

Fig. 19.4 Piece is held firmly with thumbs on top and fingers below edge. Buffing is always done below center of rotating.wheel.

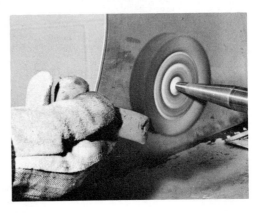

Fig. 19.5 Green buffing wheel is charged with green rouge.

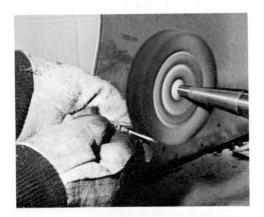

Fig. 19.6 Piece is polished to high finish with green rouge wheel.

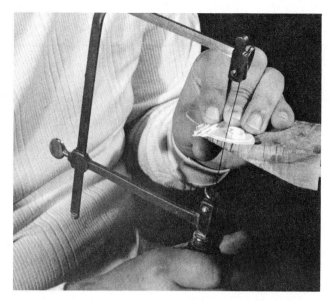

Fig. 19.7   After final soldering is completed, protruding edge is sawed off.

Fig. 19.8   Edge is sculptured with file.

Fig. 19.9   Filed edge is smoothed with emery stick prior to buffing.

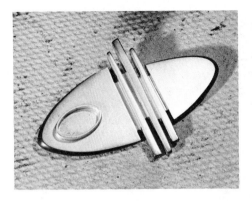

Fig. 19.10 Piece is annealed to build up fire skin in preparation for scratch buffing.

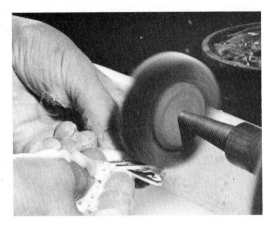

Fig. 19.11 Piece is soapy-water brushed with brass wire brush. This process of annealing and brushing is repeated three times.

After buffing, the piece is annealed. During the annealing the dark spots will turn a hazy white and the bright areas will develop a black scale. The pickle solution will remove the scale. Brushing the surface with the brass wire brush and soapy water will give the metal the lustrous look of fine silver.

In figure 19.1, a bezel is soldered to a flat surface. Because it would be difficult to polish the surface around the bezel after it has been soldered together, the surface is polished prior to the soldering. The solder is placed on the inside of the bezel and drawn out to keep the surface clean and free from solder. The edge of the piece is finished after the bezel is soldered in place. When metal is purchased, it is relatively free from scratches. Care should be used to avoid putting unnecessary scratches in metal to minimize the work of the finishing process.

Buffing wheels are important to the finishing of metal. They are, however, capable of pulling a piece of jewelry from your hands and flinging it with great force into the hood of the buffing maching with probable damage to the piece. Buffing wheels rotate down and toward the operator. To avoid accidents, keep the edge of the metal away from the buffing wheel by grasping the upper edge of the piece with the fingers below and the thumbs above the piece and allow the buffing wheel to rotate over the surface of the metal. Keep the piece moving across the surface of the buffing wheel. If the piece is not moved constantly, the buffing compounds may wear grooves in the surface. Sculptured edges and sharp, crisp lines are also easily worn away with too much buffing. When a piece is properly prepared with emery cloth, the polishing should take a very few moments.

Fig. 19.12 Flat surface of forged wire neckpiece is filed to remove hammer marks with flat or hand file.

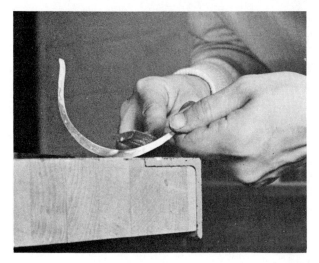

Fig. 19.13 Concave surfaces and curves are filed with the round side of a half-round file.

Fig. 19.14 Convex surfaces are filed with flat or hand file.

**108**

**Finishing**

Wire is difficult to polish on an ordinary buffing wheel because it tends to slip off the wheel surface and scratch on the arbor. Large goblet buffs offer more polishing surface and less chance of accident.

When a brightly polished piece of jewelry is oxidized, excess oxidation can be removed with a strip of suede leather cemented to a piece of wood and impregnated with green or red rouge.

On brush or scratch finish pieces, remove excess oxidation with pumice powder and restore the shine with 4/0 steel wool.

Fig. 19.15 A goblet buff offers greater surface for polishing wire forms.

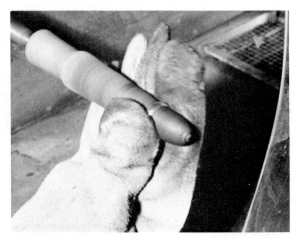

Fig. 19.16 Inner surface or ring is polished with a felt inside ring buff.

# TEXTURING

A piece or portion of a piece may be enhanced with a rough texture. This may be accomplished with the use of burrs and a flexible shaft. Different burrs will produce different textures. Vibrating tools add still other textures that can be used for additional effects.

Chasing tools come in many shapes and sizes and add unlimited possibilities for the texturing of metal. Whenever embellishments of this type are used, however, they should not be used as ornamentation for the sake of ornamentation, but rather as an integral part of the design.

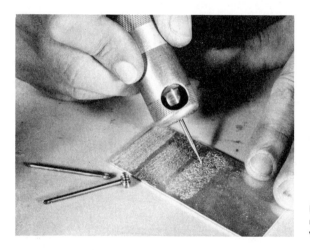

Fig. 19.17 Various textures are applied to metal surface with flexibel shaft and a variety of burrs.

Fig. 19.18 A vibrating tool offers other textural effects.

Fig. 19.19 Chasing tools create a deeper, more permanent texture.

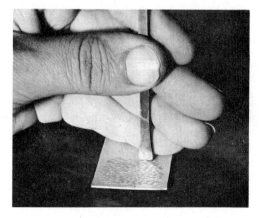

# 20 Oxidation

Oxidation can have a dramatic effect on a piece of jewelry by accenting a design or heightening the color of certain stones such as opals, moonstones, and star sapphires.

The most commonly used oxidizing agent is liver of sulphur. It is purchased in lump form and dissolved in water. The solution should be kept in a dark glass jar and it must be kept covered when not in use because both light and air will destroy the chemical properties of the solution. A lump the size of a cherry pit to 2 ounces of water will give excellent results. The solution has a rather unpleasant odor, but it is far less expensive than other commercially available oxidizing agents.

Best results are achieved when the piece of jewelry to be oxidized is heated to 212°F. This is accomplished by placing a drop of the oxidizing solution on the piece and heating it with a soft flame until the moisture begins to boil. Then remove the heat and brush the solution over the area to be oxidized. Heat the piece occasionally to maintain the 212° temperature while working.

When the piece is completely oxidized, allow it to cool, then wet it with cool water and rub pumice over the high areas to remove as much of the oxidation as you feel will best complement your design. Bring up the luster of the metal by rubbing it with very fine (3/0 or 4/0) steel wool. A very thin film of oil on the oxidized surfaces will darken them still further and give them an irridescent quality.

Fig. 20.1 Piece is laid on asbestos and gently heated with a soft flame (no air) to approximately 212$^{\circ}$F.

Fig. 20.2 Oxidation (liver of sulphur) is painted on warm piece, blackening it completely.

Figs. 20.3, 20.4 With a moistened thumb and pumice powder, highlights and subtle shading are achieved by removing the oxidation from raised areas.

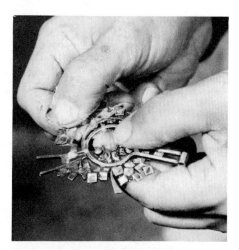

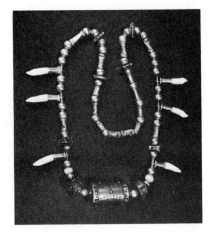

# 21 Contemporary American Jewelers

This final chapter is meant to tease and entice the novice jeweler. The artists I have chosen are all friends and contemporary American jewelers and represent a wide geographic spread from north to south and east to west. Most, but not all, of them are currently teaching. All are unique in their approach to their art and make a strong personal statement. Rather than trying to interpret them to the reader, I prefer to let them speak for themselves, both verbally and visually, in the hope that they will excite the viewer to search out further work from them and the many other excellent jewelers working throughout the country. The more fine work you see and, hopefully, handle and examine closely, the greater will be your inspiration and impetus to broaden and deepen your own exploration and development as a jeweler.

(ABOVE) EBENDORF:
Fig. 21.1 *Necklace,* copper, brass, silver, ivory, and amber; large center bead has engraved detail, silver rivets, and stamped detail; fabricated.

## ROBERT EBENDORF
*Professor, State University College at New Paltz*

EBENDORF:
Fig. 21.2 *Pin*, copper, silver, old
tintype, gold wire, and found
objects; fabricated.

EBENDORF:
Fig. 21.3 *Necklace,* silver and beads;
silver constructed beads are repoussed
and chased.

EBENDORF:
Fig. 21.4 *Pin,* metal, feather, found
object, and chain assemblage.

EBENDORF:
Fig. 21.5 *3 belt buckles,* chased, stamped,
engraved, repoussed, rivetted and pierced
surface decoration.

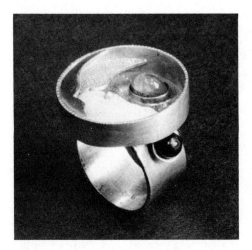

BENNETT:
Figs. 21.6, 21.7 *Ring,* with star sapphire, carved ivory, and black pearls, fabricated.

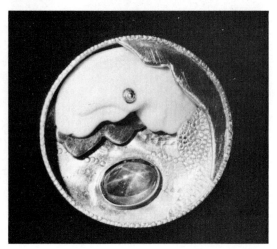

## JAMIE BENNETT
*Professor, Bradley University, Peoria, Illinois*

My first associations and pleasures with the arts developed in clay. However, I found my pieces were drying up and crumbling before I could finish my final detailing. At that, my detailing ended up being a garnishing of gems, jewels, glitters, and pearls (via Woolworth's) which was questionable for a ceramist. So, considering metal was cleaner, and gems and jewels were a commonplace, I switched. Also, I found a grand amount of tools, which amazed me, since in growing up I barely knew the existence of any beyond a hammer.

This entrancement with tools, and the metal's reflective quality to other materials continues to excite me; and the possibilities of finding new tools and more gorgeous materials to use elates me.

FISCH:
Fig. 21.8 *Pectoral,* "The Devil Himself," chased sterling silver; fabricated.

## ARLINE FISCH
*Professor, University of California/San Diego*

Looking at my recent work objectively I can see that things have assumed a quite ritualistic tone. The scale of individual ornaments, the use of beads and feathers, of faces and wings all relate to the cultures whose work I have studied in great detail—Pre-Columbian Peru, Mexico, Egypt, Africa, Eskimo, and American Indian. This has been a rather unconscious development which has been growing for the past several years. It seems to fit logically with my own needs for more humanistic and imagistic forms as well as for larger scale effects which are still comfortable to and compatible with the human form. It also somehow is an appropriate direction for the times—or so it seems to me at the moment.

FISCH:
Fig. 21.9 *Beads,* "Moroccan Memory,"
silver and amber beads; fabricated.

FISCH:
Fig. 21.10 *Collar,* "Palms," chased sterling
silver in four sections; fabricated.

FISCH:
Fig. 21.11 *Brooch,* "Birdman," 18k chased
gild and pheasant feathers; fabricated.

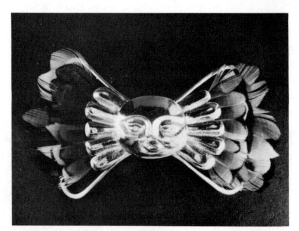

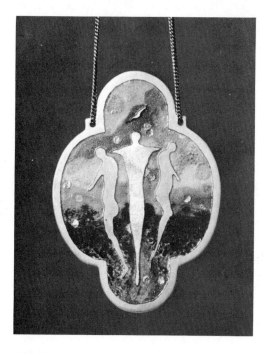 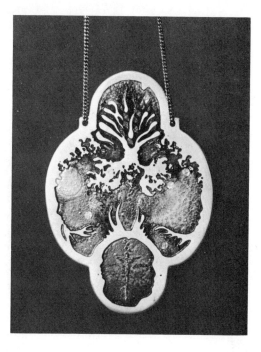

HELWIG:
Figs. 21.12, 21.13 *Pendant* (front and back views), champlevé enamel on silver-plated copper, with gold foil inlay front and back.

## HAROLD B. HELWIG
*Part-time teacher, State University College at Buffalo*

My objects are pictorial extensions of a personal mythology. Each object states its being, a blend of the internal made public. Each capsule statement in miniature is brief and direct, not meant to ornament, but introduce the viewer to the wearer.

The object is an implement of thought rather than an ornament.

My choice of material—enamel on metal

The process—fire

The reason is that I am.

HELWIG:
Fig. 21.14 *Necklace,* sterling silver and quartz with articulated wings; fabricated.

117

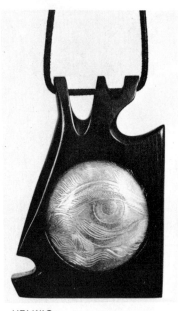

HELWIG:
Fig. 21.15 *Pendant,* basse-taille enamel set in rosewood.

HELWIG:
Fig. 21.16 *Ring,* sterling silver with basse-taille enamel dome; fabricated.

HELWIG:
Fig. 21.17 *Belt buckle,* sterling silver with champlevé enamel.

HELWIG:
Fig. 21.18 *Feelie,* carved ivory.

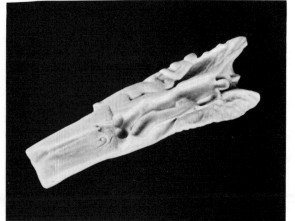

HELWIG:
Fig. 21.20 *Pendant,* Limoges
enamel set in sterling silver.

HELWIG:
Fig. 21.19 *Man's tie,* cocobola wood,
with sterling silver hinges for flexing.

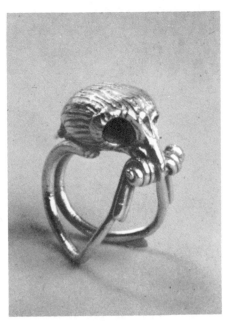

KINGTON:
Fig. 21.21 *Ring,* fantasy bird, cast 18k gold.

# BRENT KINGTON
*Professor, Southern Illinois University*

My production of jewelry is limited, as it does not serve as my primary form of expression. Normally my work is on a much larger scale. When I do make jewelry, I am confronted with three distinct problems. It is necessary that I give serious consideration to the needs and demands of the wearer. I never consider the person who wears a piece of my work as a pedestal to display miniature sculpture. Rather, I choose to view my jewelry as an adornment of the human form. I have long been fascinated with the animal-human motif that is continually recurring in historical examples of jewelry. It is in this context that I seem best able to express the humorous and satirical attitude with which I view my environment. The technical aspect finally becomes the fusing element between the two other considerations. If there is success in a piece, it comes when proper relationships are established among the three areas of concern.

KINGTON:
Fig. 21.22 *Angle pin,* cast 18k gold and 14k gold.

KINGTON:
Fig. 21.23 *Pendant,* puppet, cast 18k gold.

KINGTON:
Fig. 21.24 *Bracelet,* forged sterling silver.

**121**

KRIEGMAN:
Fig. 21.25 *Multiple-use necklace/pendant/pin,* sterling silver, cast with quartz crystal beads and chalcedony, showing various possible arrangements of components.

## CAROLYN KRIEGMAN
*Studio jeweler, part-time teacher*

"Jewelry" is an over-exercised, exhausted word, lumping together a whole gamut from meaningless multiples to encrusted, belabored protestations of wealth often reflective more of pretense to status than elegance. Many, alas, strike me more as a flexing of technical musculature than aesthetic prowess.

So I'm not at all sure I make jewelry. Ideally, I make objects small enough to be worn, that repeat my vision of beauty and exemplify my encompassing need to simplify, unravel, and unelaborate. I aspire to communicate, thereby, with such as may be my soulmates.

I'm convinced that many people surround themselves at home with objects that are very personal extensions of their identities. Hopefully, in electing to wear pieces of mine, they achieve portable images of their heartlands with which to greet a populous and anonymous world.

After spending lo, these many years figuring out who I am, my struggle is to have faith in my discovery, to be satisfied with voicing it, and to pursue its growth with singular allegiance. The quiet of my inner eye is often a challenge to attain, but the goal is always worth the winning.

KRIEGMAN:
Fig. 21.26 *Pin,* 14k gold cast pieces on sterling silver reticulated base.

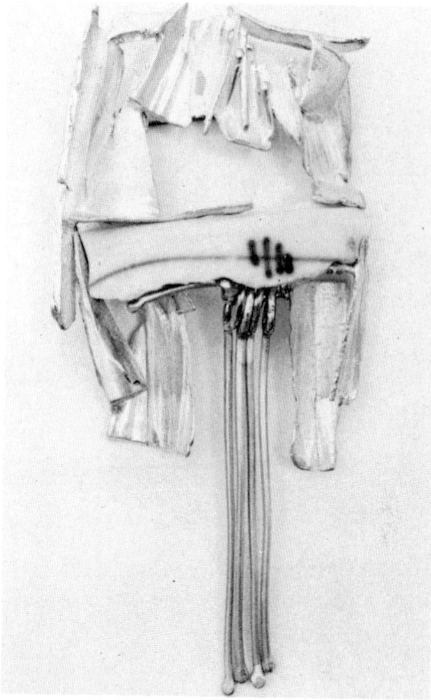

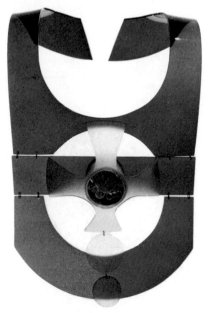

KRIEGMAN:
Fig. 21.28 *Pin,* cast sterling silver, with beach glass and baroque pearl on reticulated sheet base.

KRIEGMAN:
Fig. 21.27 *Pin,* sterling silver, with blue-and-white beach shard.

KRIEGMAN:
Fig. 21.29 *Body ornament,* plexiglas, black lucite, with clear lens which appears to move but is stationary.

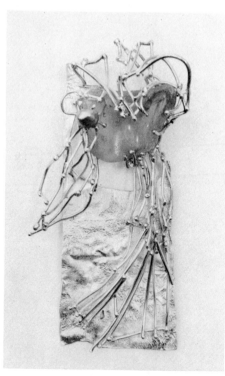

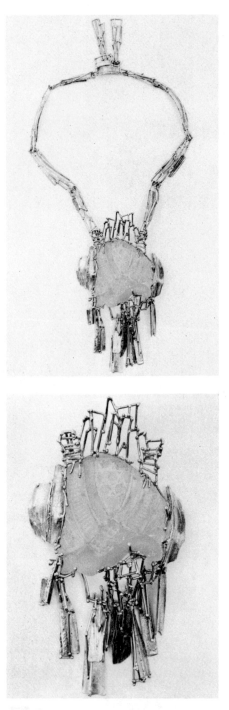

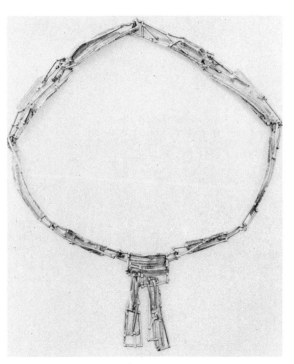

KRIEGMAN:
Figs. 21.30, 21.31, 21.32 *Multiple-use necklace/pendant/pin*,
sterling silver, showing it as necklace only, and with pendant
drop as pin.

MOTY:
Fig. 21.33 *Neckpiece,* silver gilt, rutilated quartz, and plexiglas; fabricated.

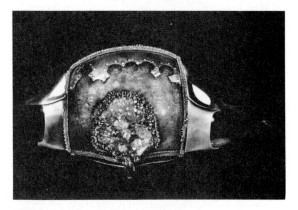

MOTY:
Fig. 21.34 *Belt with buckle,* "Dodge City Cowboy Band," photo-etched copper, with brass, garnet crystal, optic fibers, and vinyl belt.

MOTY:
Fig. 21.35 *Cameo pin,* silver, 14k gold, agate, and photo-electroplated copper.

## ELEANOR MOTY
*Professor, University of Wisconsin/Madison*

Metal and metal techniques have offered the craftsman great opportunities for aesthetic expression. In recent years, however, less emphasis has been placed upon materials of intrinsic value for jewelry and metalsmithing. Now we can feel perfectly comfortable using whatever materials (and processes) suit our aesthetic or functional needs. The creation of large-scale jewelry turning toward sculpture is encouraged by many craftsmen and accepted less reluctantly by the public.

Contemporary technology and photographic imagery have been important influences in my work and constantly indicate new and exciting possibilities. For me, designs are most often derived from a visual relationship between materials, forms, and images. Quite often the land or landscape exists somewhere in the work, but this is not always obvious. We are more inclined now to design work in the round, offering not just an interesting frontal view but also exciting discoveries in the back, inside, or other unlikely places.

MOTY:
Figs. 21.36, 21.37  *Landscape handbag*—front, silver, with silver
photo-electroplate, brass, assorted metal inlay, and agate,
fabricated; back—photo-printed leather.

MOTY:
Figs 21.38, 21.39  *Lightning box,* sterling
silver, with assorted metal inlay, brass, agate,
and photo-printed leather lining; fabricated.

126

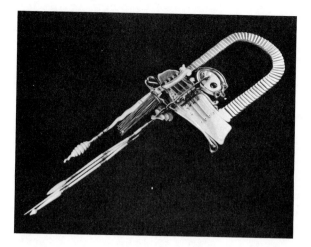

PALEY:
Fig. 21.40 *Pendant,* sterling silver, 14k gold, and copper wire, with ivory, moonstones, glass lens, and green stone; fabricated.

PALEY:
Fig. 21.41 *Pendant,* sterling silver and 14k gold, with ivory, amber, tourmaline crystal, opals, and pearls; fabricated.
*Photo by Roger B. Smith.*

## ALBERT PALEY
*Professor, State University College at Brockport*

The goldsmith is a complete anachronism in contemporary society if considered solely as a means to manufacture an object. For this the industrial revolution has superseded human dexterity, precision, and production. The mere making of an object is therefore unnecessary and unimportant unless through the working process something else is derived. The basic conceptual aspects that determine jewelry form are being systematically analyzed and questioned by several individuals who are demanding answers. The object is only the tangible manifestation and reference to this research—a byproduct of a continuum becoming obsolete and dated upon its moment of completion.

The perception of form and development of an object is an organic process, responding not only to the inherent physical character of materials and working processes but also the structural, mechanical, and conceptual considerations. Totality of the object is of prime importance, whether in conjunction with the human form or in isolation. A hierarchy does not exist between the decorative, structural, or mechanical aspects of the piece, rather an integration and acceptance of the necessary components—where a prong is of equal importance to the stone which it is holding or a brooch is as important as the contour to which it is pinned or the gesture to which it responds.

127

PALEY:
Fig. 21.42 *Brooch,* sterling silver and 14k gold, with coral, pearls, and agate; fabricated. *Photo by Roger B. Smith.*

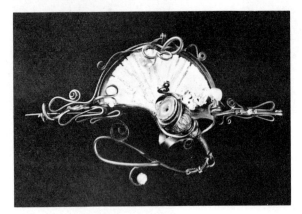

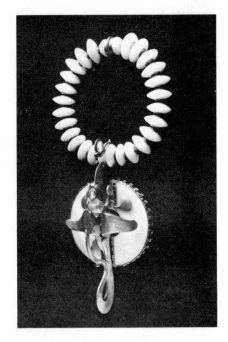

PALEY:
Fig. 21.43 *Pendant,* cooper, with 14k gold inlay, delrin, glass lens, and bead; fabricated and forged.

PALEY:
Fig. 21.44 *Pendant,* sterling silver, 14k gold, copper, with cameo, delrin, and pearls; fabricated. *Photo by Roger B. Smith.*

PALEY:
Fig. 21.45 *Pendant,* sterling silver, 14k gold, copper, with delrin, tourmaline crystal, glass lens; fabricated. *Photo by Roger B. Smith.*

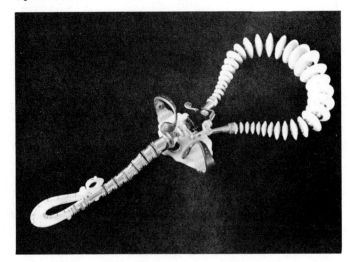

128

# MARY ANN SCHERR
*Professor, Kent State University*

SCHERR:
Fig. 21.46 *Body/air-sensor necklace,* stainless steel, liquid crystals, peacock feathers; liquid crystals measure body and air temperature; fabricated.

SCHERR:
Fig. 21.47 *Torso necklace,* 14k gold; fabricated.

SCHERR:
Fig. 21.48 *Gauntlet,* sterling silver, with Guyanese black baroque stone.

SCHERR:
Figs. 21.49, 21.50 *Oxygen mask pendant,* bio/medical body/air sensor, sterling silver and amber; photo cell senses air, which electronically triggers a sound device to alert wearer to pollution; pendant contains oxygen and mask; fabricated.

SCHERR:
Fig. 21.51 *Necklace,* 14k gold interlocking units, with 50 diamonds.

SCHERR:
Fig. 21.52 *Necklace,* 14k gold fringe.

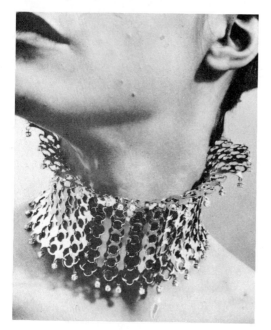

130

# OLAF SKOOGFORS
*Professor, Philadelphia College of Art*

SKOOGFORS:
Fig. 21.53 *Pendant,* gold-plated sterling
silver and ivory; fused and fabricated.

SKOOGFORS:
Fig. 21.54 *Necklace,* gold-plated sterling
silver; fabricated.

SKOOGFORS:
Fig. 21.55 *Pin,* gold-plated sterling
silver; fabricated.

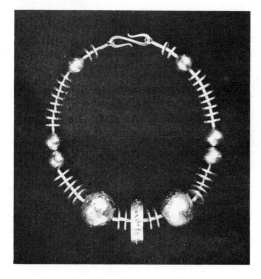

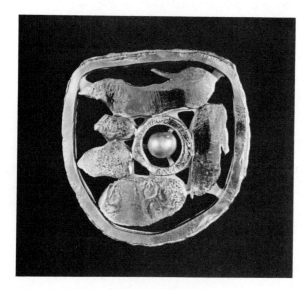

SKOOGFORS:
Fig. 21.56 *Pin,* gold-plated sterling silver, with baroque
pearl; fused and fabricated.

SKOOGFORS:
Fig. 21.57 *Pin,* sterling silver cast center section in
constructed frame.

SKOOGFORS:
Fig. 21.58 *Pin,* gold-plated sterling silver;
fabricated.

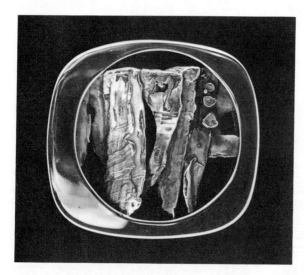

SOLBERG:
Fig. 21.59 *Necklace,* brass tags and
silver; fabricated. (Collection of Fred
Cole.) *Photo by William Eng.*

SOLBERG:
Fig. 21.60 *Necklace,* "Africa," sterling
silver, ostrich shell beans, and bone;
fabricated. (Collection of Mrs. Russell
Day.)

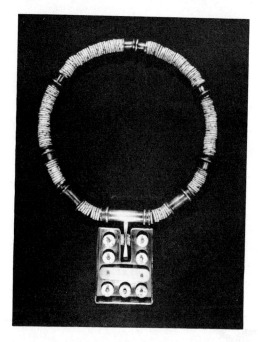

## RAMONA SOLBERG
*Professor, University of Washington/Seattle*

I am such an inveterate collector of beads and memorabilia that this is usually
my point of departure when I start designing a piece of jewelry. The question I
ask is: How can I display these collectables in a unique, wearable, well-designed
way? Relationships of shapes, patterns, and colors are constantly considered.

Since display seems to be of major importance in these pieces, my metal
techniques have remained relatively direct and unsophisticated. I usually fabri-
cate (of sheet and wire), with a modest amount of forging to enhance the metal
and complement and enhance visual qualities in the selected material. I some-
time combine silver and brass or bronze. Casting is a favorite way of making
beads and important fasteners. I also electroform to create interesting colors and
textures as well as environments surrounding unmountable objects.

I know I have been influenced by the ethnic jewelry collected on my travels,
and if I can make my statements as personal and spontaneous as these native
craftsmen, I will be a satisfied jeweler.

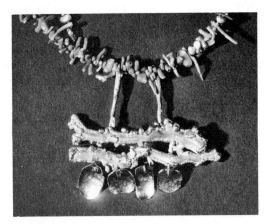

SOLBERG:
Fig. 21.62 *Necklace* (detail), branch
coral, with electroformed areas and
forged silver elements.

SOLBERG:
Fig. 21.61 *Necklace*, branch coral, with
cast silver and bronze front catch.
(Collection of Mrs. Grant Green.) *Photo
by William Eng.*

SOLBERG:
Fig. 21.64 *Necklace*, sterling silver, with stone
and clay spindle wharls and pre-Columbian
beads. (Collection of Ann O'Keefe.) *Photo by
William Eng.*

SOLBERG:
Fig. 21.63 *Necklace*, electroformed
silver, with rose quartz. (Collection of
Mrs. Herschel Roman.) *Photo by
William Eng.*

ZELMANOFF:
Fig. 21.65 *Neckpiece,* cast
sterling silver face, etched bronze,
and silver wire; fabricated. *Photo
by Peter Moore.*

# MARCI ZELMANOFF
*Studio jeweler, New York City*

I'm basically trying to make metal organic and sensual through fabrication of
fine gauge wire and other minute pieces. I want the intricate parts to add up to
form instead of being added to form. I'm also trying to get as painterly an object
as possible through combining various non-ferrous metals. I want to reach a new
feminine imagery—delicate and strong, but not imitative of masculine styles.
Since my concern is with imagery and not technique, I would hope to reach the
fine-art stature, realizing that objects that are worn have a problem divorcing
themselves from decoration.

**135**

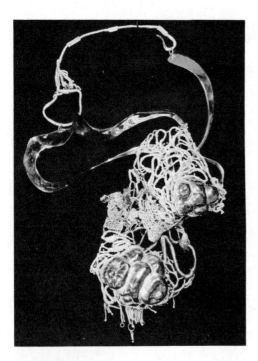

ZELMANOFF:
Fig. 21.66 *Choker,* forged and chased
sterling silver, with wrapped fine silver
wire; fabricated.

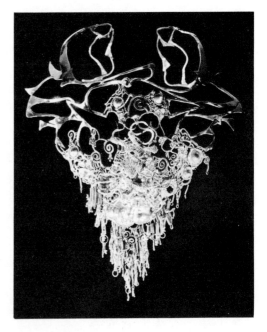

ZELMANOFF:
Fig. 21.67 *Neckpiece,* "Princess," forged
and chased sterling silver, with wrapped
fine silver wire; fabricated.

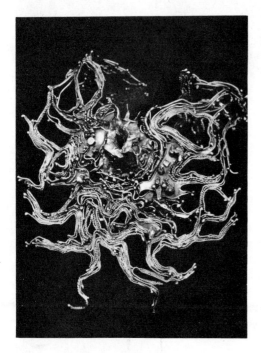

ZELMANOFF:
Fig. 21.68 *Neckpiece,* cast sterling
silver, with sterling sheet and twisted
fine silver wire; fabricated.

136

# Appendix

MELTING POINTS

*Nonferrous Metals Used in Jewelry Making*

| Platinum | 3224°F | Silver (sterling) | 1640°F |
|----------|--------|-------------------|--------|
| Gold | 1945°F | Brass | 1750°F |
| Silver (fine) | 1761°F | Copper | 1981°F |

*Silver solder*     *Gold solder*

| For fine & sterling | Melting point | Flow point | For 10K & 14K yellow gold | Flow point | For 10K & 14K white gold | Flow point |
|---------------------|---------------|------------|---------------------------|------------|--------------------------|------------|
| easy | 1260°F | 1325°F | easy 10K | 1380°F | easy 10K | 1350°F |
| medium | 1335°F | 1390°F | medium 10K | 1415°F | easy 14K | 1375°F |
| hard | 1435°F | 1435°F | easy 14K | 1390°F | | |
| I.T. | 1450°F | 1565°F | medium 14K | 1485°F | | |

## TEMPERATURE CONVERSIONS

**From Fahrenheit to Centigrade**

Subtract 32 and divide the remainder by 1.8    *Example:*

932°F

−32

900

$900.0 \div 1.8 = 500°C$

**From Centigrade to Fahrenheit**

Multiply by 1.8 and add 32.    *Example:*

$500°C \times 1.8 = 900$

900

+32

932°F

## WEIGHTS AND MEASURES

**Troy Weight**

24 grains = 1 dwt (pennyweight)
20 dwt = 1 ounce troy
12 ounces = 1 pound troy

**Avoirdupois Weight**

16 drams = 1 ounce avoir
16 ounces = 1 pound avoir
28 pounds = 1 quarter
4 quarters = 1 cwt (hundredweight)
20 cwt = 1 ton avoir

**Conversion: Troy/Avoirdupois**

Troy ounces to avoir ounces:
    Multiply by 1.09714
Avoir ounces to troy ounces:
    Multiply by 0.91146

**Carat Points**

1 carat = 100 points
½ carat = 50 points
¼ carat = 25 points

**Gram Weight**

1.555 grams = 1 dwt
31.103 grams = 1 ounce troy
28.35 grams = 1 ounce avoir

**Carat Weight**

1 carat = 3-1/16 grains troy
1 carat = .007 ounces avoir
1 carat = .20 grams

## CONVERSION OF FRACTIONS AND DECIMALS TO MILLIMETERS

| Fractions | Decimal inches | Millimeters | Fractions | Decimal inches | Millimeters |
|-----------|---------------|-------------|-----------|---------------|-------------|
| 1/32 | 0.0313 | 0.7937 | 9/32 | 0.2812 | 7.1437 |
| 1/16 | 0.6250 | 1.5875 | 5/16 | 0.3125 | 7.9374 |
| 3/32 | 0.0937 | 2.3812 | 11/32 | 0.3438 | 8.7312 |
| 1/8 | 0.1250 | 3.1750 | 3/8 | 0.3750 | 9.5249 |
| 5/32 | 0.1562 | 3.9687 | 13/32 | 0.4062 | 10.7155 |
| 3/16 | 0.1875 | 4.7624 | 7/16 | 0.4375 | 11.1124 |
| 7/32 | 0.2187 | 5.5562 | 15/32 | 0.4687 | 11.9061 |
| 1/4 | 0.2500 | 6.3499 | 1/2 | 0.5000 | 12.6999 |

## SPECIFIC GRAVITY OF METALS

Fine gold:

| | |
|---|---|
| 24kt | 19.36 |
| 18kt | 15.5 |
| 14kt | 13.4 |
| 10kt | 11.57 |
| Fine silver | 10.5 |
| Sterling silver | 10.46 |
| Bronze | 9.0 |
| Copper | 8.9 |
| Brass | 8.5 |

To determine the amount of metal needed for a casting, weigh the sprued wax model and multiply this figure by the specific gravity of the metal to be cast. If the model to be cast weighs 1 gram and sterling silver is to be used, multiply 1 by 10.46, which equals approximately 10½ grams. To be on the safe side, it is advisable to add an additional 4 or 5 grams of the metal.

# Glossary

*Alloy*   A metal that is a mixture of two or more metals. (Sterling silver is 92.5 percent fine silver and 7.5 percent copper.)

*Annealing*   A process used to heat and then cool metal to soften, make more malleable, and prevent brittleness.

*Asbestos*   A grayish mineral that is fireproof and used as insulation.

*Bezel*   A flange that holds a gem in place.

*Binding Wire*   Iron or stovepipe wire that is very flexible and is used to bind pieces of metal together when necessary for soldering.

*Buffing*   Process of polishing metal to give it a high shine.

*Cabochon*   Any precious or semiprecious stone cut in a convex shape, polished but not faceted.

*Carat*   Unit of weight for precious and semiprecious stones and pearls, equal to approximately 3.17 grains troy or 0.2 gram.

*Centrifuge*   Apparatus used to thrust molten metal into investment in casting process.

*Champlevé* Raised field in enameling process.

*Chasing* A method of applying surface decoration to metal from above with a variety of punches and hammer.

*Cheniers* The segments of tubing that comprise a hinged joint.

*Cloisonné* A form of enameling in which the surface decorations are set in hollows formed of fine silver wire.

*Cottle* A flask in which a wax model is sprued and invested for casting.

*Crucible* A refractory receptacle in which metal is placed for melting.

*Dapping* The process of forcing metal into a dome shape with use of dapping block and punches.

*Draw Plate* Instrument used for reducing gauge of wires.

*Emery Cloth* Abrasive material used in the finishing process of metal.

*Enameling* The process of fusing colored glass, both transparent and opaque, to metal with heat.

*Etching* The process of producing designs on metal with the use of acids.

*Filigree* Delicate, lacelike ornamental work of wire.

*Fire Scale* Black oxidation that forms on sterling silver and copper after heating.

*Fire Skin or Fire Coat* Coat of fine silver that remains on sterling after heating, then pickling.

*Flux* A chemical in liquid or paste form used to aid the flow of solder and impede the formation of oxides on the metal surface.

*Forging* To form or shape metal by hammering.

*Fusing* Method of joining metal with heat and without the use of solder.

*Investment* A heat-resistant plaster used to make molds for casting.

*Karat* Unit of measure which indicates content of gold in an alloy. One karat is equal to 1/12th part of pure gold.

*Kiln* Oven used by jewelers in enameling and for burnout in lost wax casting process.

*Liver of Sulphur* Potassium sulfide, a chemical used to oxidize silver, copper, and brass.

*Mica* Heat-resistant mineral silicate, transparent and in sheet form, used in plique à jour enameling.

*Oxidizing* Method of blacking areas of metal to accent a design.

*Pickle* Acid solution used to clean fire scale and flux residue that remains on metal after heating or soldering.

**142** *Planishing* Process of smoothing metals by hammering with polished hammers over metal stakes.

*Plique à Jour* Type of enameling in which enamel is fired into pierced areas of metal, permitting light to pass through the enamel and giving it a stained-glass appearance.

*Prong Setting* A method of setting faceted stones.

*Repoussé* Formed in relief, as a design in thin metal beaten up from the underside.

*Reticulation* Method of creating textural surface on silver alloy by building up a fire skin and melting the metal between the surfaces.

*Rolling* The reducing of a gauge of metal by running it through a rolling mill under pressure.

*Soldering* A method of joining metal with heat and specially prepared alloys (solder).

*Sprue* An opening through which metal flows into a mold.

*Stakes* Wood and metal forms over which metal is shaped.

*Temper* State of metal with regard to its degree of hardness and resiliency.

*Yellow Ochre* Type of soil; a mixture of clay, sand, and straw which, when mixed with water to a thin paste, becomes an insulating material used to prevent solder from reflowing.

# Bibliography

Ball, Fred, *Experimental Techniques in Enameling*. Princeton, N.J.: Van Nostrand Reinhold, 1972.

Bates, Kenneth, *Enameling Principles and Practice*. Cleveland, Ohio: World Publishing Co., 1951.

——, *The Enamelist*. Cleveland, Ohio: World Publishing Co., 1967.

Bovin, Murray, *Jewelry Making for Schools, Tradesmen, Craftsmen*. Published by the author, 1953.

Brynner, Irena, *Modern Jewelry*. New York: Van Nostrand Reinhold, 1968.

Chatt, Orville, *Design Is Where You Find It*. Ames, Iowa: Iowa State University Press, 1972.

Choate, Sharr, *Creative Casting*. New York: Crown, 1966.

——, with Bonnie De Moy, *Creative Gold and Silversmithing*. New York: Crown, 1970.

Franke, Lois, *Handwrought Jewelry*. Bloomington, Ill.: McKnight and McKnight, 1962.

**143**

**144**

Gentille, Thomas, *Step by Step Jewelry.* New York: Western Publishing Co., 1968.

Grando, Michael, *Jewelry Form and Technique.* Princeton, N.J.: Von Nostrand Reinhold, 1969.

Harper, William, *Step by Step Enameling.* New York: Western Publishing Co., 1973.

Hughes, Graham, *Modern Jewelry.* New York: Crown, 1963.

Martin, Charles, and Victor D'Amico, *How to Make Modern Jewelry.* New York: published by Museum of Modern Art, distributed by Doubleday & Co., 1949.

Maryon, Herbert, *Metalwork and Enameling,* 4th ed. New York: Dover Publications, 1959.

Pack, Greta, *Jewelry and Enameling,* 3rd ed. Princeton, N.J.: Van Nostrand, 1961.

——, *Chains and Beads.* Princeton, N.J.: Van Nostrand Reinhold, 1951.

Seeler, Margaret, *The Art of Enameling.* Princeton, N.J.: Van Nostrand Reinhold, 1969.

Shoenfelt, Joseph, *Designing and Making Handwrought Jewelry.* New York: McGraw-Hill, 1960.

Story, Mickey, *Centrifugal Casting as a Jewelry Process.* Scranton, Pa.: International Textbook Co., 1963.

Untracht, Oppi, *Metal Techniques for Craftsmen.* Garden City, N.J.: Doubleday & Co., 1968.

——, *Enameling on Metal.* Philadelphia: Chilton Co., 1961.

Von Neumann, Robert, *Design and Creation of Jewelry.* Philadelphia: Chilton Co., 1961.

Weiner, Louis, *Hand Made Jewelry.* Princeton, N.J.: Von Nostrand, 1948.

Willcox, Donald, *New Design in Jewelry.* Princeton, N.J.: Van Nostrand Reinhold, 1970.

Winebrenner, D. Kenneth, *Jewelry Making as an Art Expression.* Scranton, Pa.: International Textbook Co., 1955.

# Index

Alloy, 30, 61
Aluminum, 48
American Crafts Council, 2
Annealing, 30-32, 36, 39, 41, 49, 61, 102, 106
Annealing pan, 21, 30-31
Asbestos board, 22

Ball peen hammers, 14
Bangle bracelets, 27
Beakhorn, 38
Belt buckles, 10
Bench, jeweler's, 19
Bennett, Jamie, 114
Bezels, 27, 49, 73, 79-82, 106
Binding wire, 32, 84, 85
Bracelent rings, joining, 83-85
Bracelets, 27
Brass, 2, 41
    melting point, 137
    specific gravity of, 139
**145**    Bronze, 41

specific gravity of, 139
Buffing, 41, 102-3, 106
Build-up method of centrifugal casting, 90-91
Burnout, 94, 96
Burrs, 77, 84, 109
Butt soldering, 27-28

Cabochons, 73, 79
Carving method of centrifugal casting, 86-89
Casting, *see* Centrifugal casting
Centrifugal casting, 86-101
    build-up method, 90-91
    burnout, 94, 96
    carving method, 86-89
    casting, 96-101
    investing, 92, 94-96
    spruing, 92-93
Champlevé enameling, 50, 55-57
Charcoal block, 22
Chasing tools, 14, 82, 109

Cheniers, 84-85
Cloisonné enameling, 50, 51-54
Coat-hanger wire, 23
Copper, 30, 41, 48, 49, 61
    melting point, 137
    specific gravity of, 139
Costume jewelry, 2
Cottle, 92, 94, 96, 98
Counter-enameling, 49, 51
Craftsman, role of, 2-3
Crucible, 98
Cutting paper, design and, 6, 8

Dapping, 45-47
Design, 4-10
    cutting paper, 6, 8
    geometric forms, 10
    manmade objects, 10
    nature and, 8, 10
    for particular person, 10
    practicality of, 10
    sawing and piercing, 18-20
    sketching, 5-6
Disc cutting, 45-47
Draw plates, 33-34
Draw tongs, 34, 36
Drawing wire, 33-34
Drill bits, 36
Drilling, 20

Earrings, 102
    design of, 10
    plique-à-jour enameling, 58
Ebendorf, Robert, 112-13
Edge soldering, 23-24
Emery cloth, 24, 25, 41, 102-4, 106
Enameling, 30, 48-60
    champlevé, 50, 55-57
    cloisonné, 50, 51-54
    counter, 49, 51
    plique-à-jour, 58-60
    preparation of metals and enamels,
        49-51
    types of enamel, 48
    wet packing or inlaying, 50, 53
Etching, 55, 61, 68-73

Feathers, 2
Fibers, 2
Files, 15, 102-3
Findings, soldering, 29
Fine silver, 49, 61, 102
    melting point, 62, 63, 137
    reticulation, 61-63

specific gravity of, 139
Finishing, 30, 102-9
Fire scale, 48, 49, 104
Fire skin, 102
Fisch, Arline, 115-16
Flux, 22, 24, 25, 29, 64, 67, 74, 84, 85
Forging, 37-40
Forming hammers, 14
Fusing, 64-67

Geometric forms, design and, 10
Glass, 2, 48
Gold, 2, 41, 48, 49
    melting point, 137
    polishing, 102
    specific gravity of, 139
Gold solder, 22
    melting points, 137
Ground enamel, 48, 59

Hammers, 11, 14, 30, 38, 41
Helwig, Harold B., 117-19
Hinging, 83-85
Humidity, tools and, 15

Inlaying, 50, 53
Investing, 92, 94-96
Iron, 2, 14

Jewelers, contemporary American, 112-36
Jump rings, 35-36, 83

Karat, 22
Kiln, 50, 96
Kington, Brent, 120-21
Kriegman, Carolyn, 122-24

Lea buffing compound, 49
Liquid flux, 22, 64
Liver of sulphur, 110
Lump enamel, 48, 58, 59

Manmade objects, design and, 10
Mass-production, 2
Melting points, 62, 63, 137
Metals, specific gravity of, 139
Mica, 58
Millimeters, conversion of fractions and
    decimals to, 139
Moonstones, 82, 110

**Index**

Moty, Eleanor, 125-26

Nature, design and, 8, 10

Opals, 82, 110
Oxidation, 49, 64, 108, 110-11

Paley, Albert, 127-28
Paste flux, 22
Paste stones, 2
Pendants, 58, 92, 102
Pick, soldering, 22
Pickle, 29-32, 49, 62, 65, 75, 102, 106
Piercing, 20
Pins, 58, 92, 102
Planishing hammers, 14, 30, 38-41, 90
Plastic, 2
Platinum, 2
    melting point, 137
Plique-à-jour enameling, 58-60
Polishing, 68, 102-4, 106, 108
    enamel, 54, 56, 60
Practicality of design, 10
Prong settings, 49, 73-78

Repoussé, 61
Reticulation, 61-63, 64
Ring bands, 27, 28
Rings, 58, 102
Riveting, 49
Rolling, 41, 43

Saw blades, 15, 19, 20, 36
Saw frames, 15, 19, 20
Sawing, 18-20
Scarification, 1
Scherr, Mary Ann, 129-30
Scratch brush finish, 102, 104, 108
Screwing, 49
Shaping, 41
Sheet solder, 22
Silver, 2, 41, 48
    fusing, 64-66
    *See also* Fine silver; Sterling silver
Silver solder, 22
    melting points, 137
Sketching, design and, 5-6
Skoogfors, Olaf, 131-32
Solberg, Ramona, 133-34
Solder, 22, 137
Soldering, 21-29, 49, 106
    basic procedures, 23

butt, 27-28
edge, 23-24
findings, 29
materials and equipment, 21-23
sweat, 25-26, 55
Spruing, 92-93
Stakes, 14, 30
Star sapphires, 82, 110
Steel, 2, 14, 48
Sterling silver, 49
    annealing, 30-31
    melting, point, 62, 63, 137
    polishing, 102
    reticulation, 61-63
    specific gravity of, 139
Stone setting, 73-82
    bezels, 27, 49, 73, 79-82, 106
    prong settings, 49, 73-78
Stool, jeweler's, 19
Sweat soldering, 25-26, 55

Tattooing, 1-2
Temperature conversions, 138
Tempering, 34, 39
Texturing, 109
Third arm, 22
Tools, 11-17
    chasing, 14, 82, 109
    disc cutter, 45
    files, 15, 102-3
    hammers, 11, 14, 30, 138-41, 80
    humidity, 15
    rust, 14-15
    saw blades and frames, 15, 19, 20, 36
    soldering, 21-23
Torch, soldering, 21
Turntable pan, *see* Annealing pan
Tweezers, soldering, 22

Wax, 86-91
Weights and measures, 139
Wet packing, 50, 53
White metal castings, 2
Winding shanks, 35-36
Wire
    annealing, 32, 36
    bezel, 79-80
    cloisonné, 51
    drawing, 33-34
    forging, 37-40
    fusing, 67
    polishing, 108
    prong settings, 73-76
    straightening, 36, 43
    wax, 91

Wire solder, 22

Yellow ochre, 22

Zelmanoff, Marci, 135-36